STOPPING TIME

Paul Bley in New York, late sixties.
Photo by Sy Johnson

Stopping Time
Paul Bley

AND THE TRANSFORMATION
OF JAZZ

PAUL BLEY

WITH

DAVID LEE

Véhicule Press

Véhicule Press acknowledges the ongoing assistance of
The Canada Council for the Arts

The publisher has made efforts to obtain permission
for all copyrighted material used in this book and will be pleased to
acknowledge any missing permissions in all future editions.

Cover design by J.W. Stewart
Cover imaging by André Jacob
Cover photo by Sy Johnson
Front flap photograph by Jan Persson.
Back cover photograph by Mark Miller.
Special assistance: Len Dobbin
Typeset in Bembo by Simon Garamond
Printed by AGMV-Marquis Inc.

02 01 00 99   4 3 2 1

Dépôt légal, Bibliothèque nationale du Québec and
the National Library of Canada, 4th quarter 1999

CANADIAN CATALOGUING IN PUBLICATION DATA

Bley, Paul, 1932–
Stopping time : Paul Bley and the transformation of jazz

Includes discography and index.
ISBN 1-55065-111-0

1. Bley, Paul, 1932– 2. Jazz musicians–Canada–
Biography. I. Lee, David. II. Title

ML417.B647A3 1998   786.2'165'092   C98-900621-2

Published by Véhicule Press
vehiculepress.com

Distributed in Canada by GDS.
Distributed in the U.S. by LPC Group

Printed in Canada on alkaline paper

Contents

Acknowledgements

PAUL BLEY

This book could not have been realized without the help of David Lee who initiated this project over a decade ago; Carol Goss, who helped me see it through to completion; Simon Dardick, for his meticulous production; Len Dobbin, who kept track of my early years; Sy Johnson, for his sensitive eye; and Nancy Marrelli, for her diplomacy.

DAVID LEE

Maureen Cochrane's help was invaluable during the early stages of this manuscript: editing, proofing, and even transcribing the tapes of the first interviews on which this book is based. The Canada Council's Explorations Program allowed me to develop a first draft, and a travel grant from its Arts Awards Services enabled me to polish a later draft with Paul Bley in Cherry Valley. Many friends offered editorial and other support, but Les Fowler, Mark Miller, Al Neil, Mary Schendlinger and Bill Smith have been called upon the most often over the years.

Paul and Betty Bley, Montreal, 1940s.

1

The Early Years

In my old neighborhood in Montreal, iron staircases go up the fronts of all the houses. Whoever thought of this really should have thought twice about it, because Montreal winters are cold, and sometimes these stairs turn into three flights of solid ice.

In the summer, however, they become everyone's front yards, and during the hot, humid summers, people spend a lot of time out on these staircases.

At the age of five I was sitting on the iron staircase in front of our house. I remember that I was holding a piece of the green crêpe paper that they used to wrap oranges in. My neighbor Esther Goldstein was playing on the stairs next door. We were talking back and forth, when suddenly in the course of our conversation Esther mentioned something about me being adopted.

"No," I laughed, "I'm not adopted!"

"You are too!"

"I am not!" We bantered about this for a few minutes, then I headed back inside and found my mother.

"Mom," I said, "Esther says I was adopted."

My mother fell into a profound silence.

I thought, "My god, Esther was right!" Then my mother said, "Well, you should love me even more now that you know."

I don't know where in the world she got that idea—or why she and my father Joe had decided not to tell me that I was adopted, but as soon as I heard my mother's response, I think I left home—in my mind, anyway. From then on, I felt that I was just biding my time until I could buy the ticket.

My mother, Betty Marcovitch, came to Montreal from Romania when she was nine years old, to join her stepfather who was running a store on Craig Street. Betty was a very hard worker, and by the time she was fifteen she had earned enough money to send for her older sister Esther. Esther eventually married in Montreal and had two sons, Hy and Frank Engel, who were to help me out greatly later in life.

Betty met and fell in love with a young man, Louis Cohen. After a whirlwind courtship they married. However, parents had a lot to say about their children's destinies in those days, and Louis' mother thought that the circumstances of a Romanian immigrant were far too modest. She had bigger plans for her son, and she had the marriage annulled.

Betty was heartbroken. Soon afterwards she met Joe Bley, a prosperous businessman who owned a factory that did embroidery work. They married, but to their dismay they were unable to have children, so they decided to adopt. The story that my mother always told me was that she came to the adoption center looking for a girl, but that as soon as she came across me I stretched my arms out and said "Mama." I guess I was a hustler even then! She picked me up and, as she always said with a great deal of passion, once she picked me up she felt she could never put me down.

At that time Joe Bley was doing very well and he was hiring employees, primarily French Canadian women. One of them, Lucie, became my nanny. She was a charming young woman and I was very much attached to her. Things were going Joe's way. He would

Paul Bley, age 13, playing with Danny Birman
at the Castle des Monts, Ste–Agathe, Quebec, 1945.
John Gilmore Fonds, Concordia University Archives

Paul and Joe Bley, Ste-Agathe, Quebec.

bring home a new car every year. I remember him demonstrating, with great pride, the floor shift on the new Packard. However, it was still the Depression and by the time I was seven, Joe's business started to decline. One night when Joe and Betty were attending the theatre, Betty ran into her first love, Louis Cohen. They decided that they couldn't go on without each other.

So my parents divorced. That was traumatic enough. Then, without warning, my mother remarried. It all happened very quickly. One night there was a different guy at the head of the supper table. I kept looking at him, looking at her, and I said to myself, "What's going on? Who is this guy? Why is he sitting at my table?" The answer was: Finish your supper. He was just there. Furthermore, he continued to be there from then on.

There was no introduction, there was no preparatory work, there was no bringing me a present; he just appeared. I hadn't yet gotten over the shock of learning that I was adopted, and now even my adoptive father was gone. I felt utterly alone.

In 1992, fifty-three years later at the age of sixty, I was taking a break between sets at Sweet Basil on Seventh Avenue in the Village, when a young man walked in and introduced himself as my cousin, Jonathan Bley. He was a classical pianist from the New York City branch of the family. Jonathan mentioned rather casually that his grandfather, my father's brother, had passed on the family lore that my father was my *real* father and that my French nanny was my *real* mother. I didn't believe him.

A couple of years later, while playing the Festival International de Jazz de Montréal, old friend and jazz radio host, Len Dobbin, mentioned that he'd met a ninety-three-year-old guy who claimed to be the lawyer at my adoption. I booked lunch with him and he told me that my father had been his friend. According to him Betty was unable to have children. Joe had an affair with a young

French Canadian woman named Lucie. When Lucie became pregnant, Joe convinced her to place me in an orphanage, where he took Betty to "pick me out." I was amazed when he confirmed this story, though it reinforced my emotions.

In the Bible, Ruth put the baby Moses in the basket, and sent him down the Nile to his fate. But not wanting to leave him, she followed Moses into the families that adopted him, and watched over him from afar. I say this because as soon as I entered the Bley household, Lucie was hired as my nanny.

So for the first five years of my life, Lucie lived in my house. She was, of course, very affectionate, and long into my adult years I wondered why the favorite people in my childhood were Lucie and my father. Of course, they were my blood parents and my mother was not. I don't think my mother ever knew the whole truth about the situation.

But being the remarkable woman that she was, Betty didn't let doubt stop her from taking charge of my education, and seeing that I pursued a career that she approved of.

Paul Bley, age two.

2

The Kindness of Others

FROM THE MOMENT I was told I was adopted I immersed myself in music. My childhood had instantly evaporated. We had a three-quarter upright piano in the house and I would spend hours at it, playing by ear all the big band recordings that I liked—the Woody Herman Orchestra, for example.

In Romania, being a musician had high status, so at age six my mother started me on violin lessons. I never liked the violin because it hurt my fingers. Nevertheless, I persevered and the next year I was giving student recitals, playing the "Hungarian Gypsy Prize Dance." Then my mother divorced my father. That shock, playing an instrument that wasn't my idea, plus attending Hebrew school in addition to public school, resulted in a kind of nervous breakdown. I was just seven years old.

I insisted on switching to piano. Later I joked that I just wanted to sit down, and in some larger sense perhaps that was true. One way or another, I needed to rest, and I found the piano less stressful. In fact, the piano was what kept me sane throughout my childhood.

I had numerous teachers. The most memorable was August Décarie, from the Paris Conservatory, who suggested I play with a glass of water on each wrist to develop good hand positions. He was a revelation. One day I asked if he would play a piece of his choice all the way through for me. It was the first time that I had ever heard someone "make music" as opposed to play notes. It was at that moment that I decided to be a pianist.

Besides going to school, I was beginning to study for my Bar Mitzvah, which required me to sing a text in Hebrew. When I asked my Rabbi "How does the melody go?" he said, "You just make it up." This was very easy for me to do. Since they neglected to translate any of the Hebrew text so that I could understand what I was singing, I could fully concentrate on making beautiful melodies as an improviser.

Up to this time I could play by ear all the written music and the improvised music I had heard, but I had not yet attempted to improvise at the piano. The Bar Mitzvah freed me by giving me permission to create spontaneous music in front of an audience. To this day I still sing while I play piano.

At that time I attended the McGill Conservatory and the Quebec Conservatory, where I studied solfège and keyboard harmony. These schools were the great believers in studying, in much detail, the three Bs: Bach, Beethoven, and Brahms. I was also employed as the rehearsal pianist for the annual variety show at the local YMHA. This gave me a working knowledge of popular music. It would be years before I learned that most popular music is almost the same song. One only had to remember the small differences; for example, most popular music consists of 32 bars in four sections of AABA of which only the B section is different. So it is really an endless series of A sections repeated ad infinitum.

As a result of my work with the Variety gang, I was hired to play dances, and got my first steady job at a summer resort in Ste. Agathe, Quebec, as a sideman with bandleader Blackie Herman. The other members in the band were much older and they taught me the ways of the world. Even though resorts are full of single girls, I remember locking myself up in the auditorium during the afternoons and composing long pieces, of which only a few fragments remain in manuscript form.

By the time I was fourteen, I had my own bands and was making a name for myself in Montreal. I used the name "Buzzy Bley" as a bandleader and had the initials "BB" on all my lighted bandstands. I became accustomed to handling large sums of money—say, $200—on behalf of a band, and hiring, rehearsing, and paying guys who were twice my age to play with me. I was tall for my age, as well, which helped jump-start my career.

When my band finished at midnight in Ste. Agathe I could go hear Al Cowan and his Tramp Band—B.T. Lundy on tenor saxophone, Buddy Jordan trumpet, Walter Bacon on drums, and Al Cowan on washboards. At the time, they were the number one jazz band in Montreal, and they always invited me to sit in. In fact, the band more or less adopted me. I had uncles who weren't as nice to me as the Tramp Band and the other black musicians in Montreal at that time.

The tradition represented by the Tramp Band belongs very much to another era. The leader dressed up in a tramp suit and played washboard. That's an old culture. These people were wonderful musicians. Some of them had played with Duke Ellington. Then they made the fatal mistake of coming to Montreal as bachelors. There was so much less racial prejudice in the French community than there was anywhere else on the continent, that what they thought was going to be a three-month gig turned out to be the beginnings of marriage, family, and domesticity.

Among Japanese shakuhachi players, when the student begins his studies he moves in with the family of the master. Similarly in the black community, if you were serious about learning their music, you would be adopted by the community and welcomed into their employment circle. It was also the only way for knowledge to be passed down from one generation to the next. You would be

Summer gig at the Chalet Hotel, Ste. Agathe, mid–1940s.
Paul Bley (piano) with Billy Graham(drums),
Tony Amor (alto sax), and Gaston Charron (bass).

encouraged to play with them, even though there was no comparison musically between your level and theirs. They were the professionals, I was the novice.

The social climate was completely reversed from what it is now. I was in my teens, tall for my age, staying up till four in the morning going to Montreal's Café St. Michel to play with Steep Wade and his contemporaries. The Café St. Michel was downtown on St. Antoine Street. The habitués were men who were professional gamblers or pimps—but I could be there at four or five in the morning, and no one *ever* bothered me. It was an after-hours club, and in Montreal in those days after hours meant *after hours*. It meant starting at three a.m. The American gamblers would come up to Montreal, because it was an open city, right into the fifties and sixties. One night, a gambler walked up to the piano, put a hundred dollar bill in the cup and said, "Keep playing, kid."

"What does he mean by that?" I asked the waiter, "Keep playing, kid'? What the heck is that supposed to mean?"

The waiter said, "It means: Keep. Playing. Kid."

That's what I was there for, so it was no problem. But the next time a hundred dollar bill appeared in my cup, it was a gambler's girlfriend who put it there. She gave me a smoldering look that suggested that she and I were going to conspire to deceive the gambler. I was young, but I wasn't stupid! I knew that this was a lose/lose situation. I sweated out that gig for weeks, knowing that if I was nice to her, she'd tell the truth, and if I wasn't nice to her, she'd lie! Eventually someone else caught her eye and I was off the hook. There was sawdust on the floor and a red light over the door, but I was safe because I belonged to the band. In fact, the atmosphere was incredibly warm and hospitable.

This was the tail end of the dance band period. Maynard Ferguson was showing up every band that came to Montreal. No matter who came to town—Tommy Dorsey, Gene Krupa, whoever—

Maynard's band was hotter and no matter who the lead trumpeter was, Maynard could play an octave higher. Their agent took great pride in having them open for famous bands and make the headliners look bad.

It was at this time, around 1948, that I had the privilege of hearing a jazz piano genius in person. Oscar Peterson, along with bassist Ozzie Roberts and drummer Clarence Jones, who had come up from New York City, were working at the Alberta Lounge six nights a week for a year. Oscar had a mirror suspended over the keyboard so that you could see his fingers move, which was a sight to remember. His talent was full blown. He had already completed his boogie-woogie period on RCA Canada and was playing at the top of his game when Norman Granz showed up one night. The word had already spread to the United States and Granz hired him on the spot to join his Jazz at the Philharmonic Tours and NorGran Records, later known as Verve Records. Both he and Maynard had something to offer the world as teenagers. That is amazing.

Now and then in the music you'll get a Tony Williams, who bursts onto the scene when he's hardly more than a boy, but that doesn't happen ten times a decade; you're lucky if it happens once a decade. It's one of the great phenomena of jazz that you can have a seventy-year-old next to a teenager, and they're relating in every possible way.

The second most charming man I have ever met, next to Duke Ellington, was Oscar. Besides being an excellent singer, he was always very supportive of me, and when he learned that he would be leaving Canada, he asked if I would replace him and finish out the contract at the Alberta Lounge with his bassist and drummer. This was 1949 and I was just beginning my final high school year. Knowing a window of opportunity when I saw one, and in spite of the fact that I was unqualified to sit in his chair, I accepted.

The following summer I began working at the Chalet Hotel

in Ste. Agathe with a singer from New York named Nina Grey. We became fast friends and I told her of my desire to live in New York City and go to Juilliard.

A young musician can count himself lucky if his parents stay out of his way. My mother did much more than that. For my seventeenth birthday she put $500 in my hands and said, "Go to New York and when you run out of money come back."

I checked into the Taft Hotel and kept my head up for a whole weekend. I concluded that I definitely liked it. Nina was convinced that there was nothing else I could possibly do and she did everything she could to help me. That September she invited me down to her home in Brooklyn. I stayed in an apartment with her and her three brothers. We ate three huge meals a day and kept rifles for Israel under the beds. Her family was wonderfully warm and attentive.

I owe a lot of what I've done to the support of the women in my life. Both Nina and my mother, Betty, were very supportive. I had a life and a circle of friends in Montreal, and I doubt very much if I would have been able to tear myself away if both of them hadn't supported my desire to leave.

3

Parker – Mingus – Young
Armstrong – Tristano

IT WAS 1950 when I left Montreal to attend the Juilliard School of Music in Manhattan. The 52nd Street scene was already in decline, but on my first night in New York I heard two bands that I'd never heard in person before. One was Charlie Parker with Max Roach, Miles Davis, and Tommy Potter on bass. After two sets of that we went down the street to hear Lennie Tristano, Lee Konitz, Warne Marsh, Billy Bauer, Peter Ind, and Al Levitt, playing all these incredible charts. Dizzy Gillespie's orchestra was at Birdland, and Billy Eckstine's orchestra was upstairs at Bop City. This was all in a four-block radius. If you went slightly further afield there was even more.

When I first checked into the Juilliard School of Music, which at the time was on the upper west side where the Manhattan School of Music is now, I found an ad on the bulletin board from Juilliard students who were looking for a roommate. I moved into an apartment with three composers and the landlady, who cooked and cleaned for us. These composers, who had graduated from Juilliard, papered the walls of their rooms with symphony scores. This way they could read the scores without having to turn pages. They were a very unhappy lot. They had graduated from Juilliard without hearing any performances of their work. The landlady was grossly overweight and very dour.

When I happened to run into Bob Reisner, who was the jazz critic for the *Village Voice* at the time, I told him about my un-happiness.

Bob said, "Paul, you're living in the wrong part of town. Why don't you move downtown to the Village? I have a big apartment; you're welcome to come and stay with me for awhile until you find a place of your own."

I said, "Bob, you're saving my life."

What was about to happen was the beginning of one of the happiest chapters of my life, which, unbeknownst to me, would last for thirty plus years—the move to Greenwich Village.

Bob had an apartment over the Art Theater on West 8th Street, nicely furnished. He told me not to be surprised if the next day someone came over. I was to just let him in. So at one o'clock the next day there was a knock at the door and there was a guy with an acoustic guitar.

He said "Bob said it was okay for me to come over."

It turned out that Bob had hired this guitar player to come over to his apartment five afternoons a week to play unaccompanied guitar to keep the apartment company. This was the beginning of a lifelong collection of characters I was to come across whose behavior was considerably different from what I'd been used to.

On my first day in composition class at Juilliard, the teacher, Henry Brant, brought out a box full of radios and passed them around the class. He taught us four signs—turn them on, turn them off, turn them up, turn them down—and proceeded to conduct a piece for twenty-one radios.

And this was just my first day! It was fascinating to be involved in music as a process of creating structure in real time, as opposed to the endless reshuffling of numerical relationships that is usually referred to as "composition." It was a much, much better way of teaching than my earlier experiences at the Montreal conservatories, which were all about rules.

We learned something about the evolution of classical music, which had gone through a parallel sequence of development 75 years earlier than jazz. Once you realized that, you could look at the history of this European art music to see what was coming next in jazz. It was easy in 1950 to see that the music was about to become very impressionistic, and so it did with the work of Miles Davis, Gil Evans, and Lennie Tristano. Even the string arrangements for Bird were highly impressionistic.

After impressionism, atonality was next. The big mystery wasn't whether atonal music was coming; it was why it wasn't already here. European music had been atonal since the twenties—what was taking jazz so long? In this regard, classical music threw us a curve, because it led us to assume that this breakthrough would be made by composers.

In jazz, the composers were generally inept pianists, which is why they had to become composers. In short, a composer is just somebody who can't play in real time.

Society accepts and forgives the fact that it takes a "serious composer" a month to create three minutes of music. But if you're an artist who loves creating music, you'd rather play it all in three minutes and then play something totally different for another three minutes. Rather than sitting up in bed with an idea, scratching it down on paper, then going through months of writing and orchestrating and copying and rehearsing before you or anyone else can hear it.

Besides, notation is full of liabilities. The accents, the phrasing—with a touch-controlled instrument—every phrase, every note within a phrase, has a radically different meaning. Some parts of a phrase are meant to be played clearly, other parts are meant to be played obscurely. How do you notate something to be played obscurely? There's just no room on the paper.

Up until the fifties, all jazz music was played on compositions that, if they weren't always popular songs, followed the song form itself. But this form is based on redundancy. If it takes a minute to play an AABA section, you've already played three redundancies in the first minute. To keep that up for fifteen minutes, with three A's per minute, is a redundancy to the highest power. We all knew this in the 1950s, but we didn't know what to do about it. Improvisers had yet to concede that since the largest part of their performances was made up, the next natural step was to eliminate the disparity between the length of the written music and the length of the improvised music. If a score was going to give you two minutes of written music in a fifteen-minute performance, why bother? Especially if it was two minutes of written music that was harmonically full of repetition.

In the early fifties, it was very difficult to see this. Composers were tying themselves up with hopeless make-work like orchestrating Bird solos, so that you had piccolo versions of Charlie Parker music that everybody could play or at least make some semblance of playing. If that wasn't the next step, what was?

One would have thought that someone would have come up with something during my four years at Juilliard. Phil Woods and Teo Macero were there at the same time I was. Teo had an orchestra at the school and Phil played in it. I never joined, although I guested in it occasionally. After all my professional experience in Montreal I couldn't see myself in a student orchestra. However, as far as atonality went, we were all up against the same wall.

Lennie Tristano's music sounded like it *might* be atonal, because it sounded so different from the most modern player we all knew, Bird. Bird was more triadic than we like to remember. He placed a great emphasis on the flatted fifth and the raised ninth, and these intervals sounded so dissonant at the time that it seemed that Bird's playing might be a major signpost on the road to atonality. Of course, now those intervals are all considered normal parts of the lower triad.

Nothing is more difficult than trying to literally force a music beyond its own limitations. I know, because I've tried. But here we were in New York trying to force jazz into atonality. It was a concern shared by all of the orchestral writers—George Russell, Gil Evans, and Johnny Carisi. If there had been, for example, an alto saxophone soloist in any of their bands who could equal what they were trying to do, that saxophonist would have become the man of the hour. But the ideas stayed in the score, because as soon as the alto saxophone player stood up to solo, it was Bird again, and didn't refer to any of the advances that were being made in the writing. You couldn't really blame the players. It was easier to write that way than it was to improvise that way.

Later on at Juilliard, I joined an organization called the New Jazz Society. They had Sunday meetings at the Downbeat Club on West 54th Street, where Bird played on weekends and Charles Mingus played during the week. Mingus came to some of the meetings, and at some point I sat in with him on one of his weeknight gigs. Mingus was very friendly towards me when I sat in, and I guess he filed me somewhere in the back of his mind.

Between 1950 and 1953, I was back and forth between New York and Montreal quite a lot. One day while I was walking down Mountain Street in Montreal, I noticed this brass plaque on the outside of a building: "Film Studio." I took a sharp right through the door and started talking to the first person I met about this great idea I had, to make a film about jazz. I thought we could get Stan Kenton to narrate it. In about twenty minutes we put together

Production shot of the Bley Trio sequence for the *Canadian Cameo Series—Spotlight No.5.* Director Gordon Sparling with Bley and bassist Neil Michaud, 1953.

Jazz Workshop, Montreal, February 1953.
Brew Moore (tenor sax) and Paul Bley (piano).
Photo by Len Dobbin.

an agreement. They got hold of Kenton's agency in New York and booked him, we agreed on a host and I appeared in the film with my trio. The director was Gordon Sparling, a pioneer Canadian documentary filmmaker.

It was plain to me that there was a level of interaction in New York that was missing in Montreal. In 1951, I got together with a couple of other Montreal pianists, Keith White and Art Roberts, and talked about the idea of a jazz workshop modeled after theatre workshops, that would give musicians the chance to practice their craft and try out new ideas with musicians imported from New York City.

The Jazz Workshop was an educational experience, completely musician-run. There were no non-musicians helping with the administration or any of the concerts. The local musicians in the Workshop were bassists Neil Michaud, Hal Gaylor, and Bob Rudd.

Billy Graham and Bobby Malloy were the drummers and other pianists included Valdo Williams and Steep Wade.

I would come up to Montreal from New York for the workshops, which were fairly frequent. Our first concert was a matinee at one of the bigger clubs, Chez Paree on Stanley Street. We got together eleven or twelve bands. We took out our expenses for publicity and transportation and paid each of the players some pocket money from admissions. We pooled the rest of it to finance the next event. At every event, all the workshop members played on the same bill, and the concerts were packed, so every club-owner in town was dying to have a Jazz Workshop event in his or her place. The bank account had nowhere to go but up. In a couple of months, there was enough money to start bringing in some outside talent.

Of course, the whole idea of doing this would be that we would play with the American guests. The first guest was guitarist Chuck Wayne, who had been playing with George Shearing. The

Workshop also brought in Sonny Rollins, Kai Winding, Jackie McLean, and Art Taylor. Then, in February 1953, we presented Brew Moore on tenor saxophone, Dick Garcia on guitar, and Charlie Parker on alto saxophone.

As soon as we brought these people up we started getting a lot more attention. The CBC offered us a series of television shows, which we did every Thursday night for a month or two. Included in this series was a half hour of Charlie Parker, on February 5, 1953, which was later released on the Uptown Records CD *Montreal 1953*. The rest of the album was taken from our Jazz Workshop concert with Bird two days later. I played piano with Bird on tracks 9 through 12 with Neil Michaud on bass, Ted Paskert on drums, and Dick Garcia on guitar. Brew Moore, tenor saxophone, joined us on tracks 10 and 12.

Getting Bird to Montreal was interesting. In New York at that time, there were a lot of private sessions, in basements and, as happened later in the seventies, in lofts. At the time though, loft sessions were not open to the public. For six months or a year there would be one or two lofts that everyone attended—Joe Albany, Charlie Parker, Red Rodney. While I was at Juilliard, I had been to a few sessions at one of these lofts, and a couple of times Bird had been there. Although we had never really spoken, this experience was sufficient to get me elected as the one who could bring Bird back alive, because he had a reputation for being unpredictable.

I had his address. Everybody lived in a basement in those days, and I remember those basements—particularly Joe Maini's. Joe was an alto saxophonist who had written out all the heads of the bebop tunes that weren't available anywhere else. They weren't published anywhere, people just played them. I would go to Joe's basement at five in the afternoon to copy charts, and there would be eight guys lying on cots in semi-darkness, with just a small red light bulb overhead.

"Joe, why is everyone asleep?"

"They're tired."

It was very much a junkie society, and at times like that, I felt like a tourist. Nevertheless, I didn't hesitate to go to New York and knock on Bird's door. But when I knocked, I heard my father's voice answering. The door opened and it was Bird. Like Joe Bley, he was a short, stout man and he had a deep, resonant voice like my father's, so he immediately became a paternal figure for me. However, I knew that I wasn't going to be adopted into his family the way I had been with the players in Montreal. The New York jazz world was a far tougher milieu. The young musicians didn't consider themselves disciples, and the knowledge of the older musicians was for sale only. If I wanted Charlie Parker to play with me, I had to hire him.

I had heard enough stories about Bird to know that if you took him to an airport and went to make a phone call, that was a mistake. So I stayed with him all the time. I took him to the plane, we traveled together, I put him in his hotel. At the end of the job I knew that I was going to have to take Bird back to New York because I didn't want him winding up in Alaska. So after the gig I took him back to New York and placed him at the door of his basement. I didn't want to be the man who lost Charlie Parker.

Drugs, of course, produce a euphoria. He would see a park or a bird he liked and he would just go to it. Plus, he was so constituted that he could keep imbibing and still function. This was another thing about some New York players. When Sonny Rollins came to the Jazz Workshop, he sat down at the table at ten o'clock at night and chugalugged a whole bottle of Gordon's Gin before the first set. The goal I was pursuing was so far off, and so difficult, that whatever accomplishments I managed to pull off along the way weren't in themselves important. It was the process that was important. I was

Bley's first released recording, *Introducing Paul Bley,*
made for Charles Mingus' label, Debut Records, 1953.
Cover photo by Alfred Wade.
Courtesy of Debut Records/ Fantasy Inc.

busy discovering what I didn't know. That was the name of the game: what I *couldn't* do—identifying an area that was a mystery to me and then taking however long it took to overcome it. This became one of my basic *modus operandi*. If I was successful in one part of the world, I'd leave immediately, and go try it somewhere else, to test if that approval was warranted.

Eventually, when Charles Mingus called—he preferred to be called Charles—even though I was working two steady jobs I basically dropped the phone and was out the door. I think that's the most important part of managing one's talent: having the judgment to know which is the important offer. And of course, I knew that if I didn't make the right choices, I'd never learn to play well enough so that Bird would call me.

Until bebop, jazz was a trumpet music, then a saxophone music, but never a piano music. It was only when Lenny Tristano arrived that the piano became a source of innovation, which would be copied by saxophonists and trumpet players.

Including Bud Powell, bebop piano was a right-handed music. They'd make a few jabs with the left hand, and call that accompaniment, but as for solos, just listen to the classic bebop records, including Bird's. When it was time for the piano solo you could go out and have a smoke until the horns came back. I came from the Oscar Peterson world where the standard was three-handed piano.

Eventually, Bird *did* call me. The voice on the phone was Dick Garcia, but Bird had asked him to hire me. I had been working for some months in Brooklyn with Pete Brown—a jump alto saxophone player in whom I saw amazing similarities, in tone and rhythmic approach, to Charlie Parker.

"Jump" is a style unique to the alto saxophone, of which Louis Jordan, the alto player and bandleader with the Tympany Five, was one of the leading exponents. Later on, it was personified by the work of Cannonball Adderley, and more recently, by Arthur Blythe. Pete Brown and Louis Jordan brought the beginnings of a style that enveloped Charlie Parker and these other alto players. Pete was considered a blues player, and Bird of course, played bebop with a great deal more complexity, but the tone and the sound were identical, and rhythmically they ran eighth notes the same way. It was amazing to be on the bandstand with these two horn players on the same evening.

Pete Brown's favorite device as a bandleader was that, if he was playing in Brooklyn in January in below-zero weather, for the first number he'd call "52nd Street Theme" as fast as he could play it. Willie Jones, the drummer, would say, "Man, why do you want to hit with that for your opening tune? Give me a chance to warm up!"

Pete would say, "If you can play this tune you'll have no more problems for the rest of the night."

I was working with him in Brooklyn on Friday, Saturday and Sunday, until midnight. Dick asked me if I'd come Saturday night and play with Bird in an armory up in Harlem beginning at one a.m. So I worked until 11:30 and then went up to play with Bird.

Bird was nowhere to be found at one a.m. We played the first set for forty minutes. Bird was nowhere to be found at two a.m. We played the second set. At three a.m., exactly, Bird walked into the Armory, unpacked as if it was midnight, and of course no one said a thing, because sixteen bars into his first chart, it *was* midnight. Nobody remembered that he was late.

That was a kind of a self-test that the great musicians gave themselves in that period. They always came very late to gigs. Other than the fact that they might have had trouble getting to the job on time, this was a test of their abilities: to play so well when they began that the audience forgot that they were two hours late. Just as several decades later, you could be allowed a hostile attitude about yourself and your work and everyone around you, provided that your great playing justified this attitude. But if your playing did not justify the attitude then you were dismissed as being a fake. In short, you have to be able to afford your attitude.

With Bird's concept, he would be playing a 32-bar tune and in the second eight, he would already be starting something that was going to get him into the bridge. Meanwhile, I was busy on bar three-and-a-half of the second eight, and in my conception of it, the bridge was a long way off.

That was a very important lesson to learn. You never play where you are. You play where you're going. Thinking ahead. Some could think ahead 16 bars, some could think ahead four choruses. Now I've gotten to the point where I can hear a whole solo in advance—not note for note, but structurally. I get an idea, facing a rhythm section or a particular instrument in a particular environment, of what can be done in what length of time.

In hearing Bird's ability to anticipate what was coming and always thinking ahead, I've tried to extend that idea to listening for three things before I start playing a phrase:

One: What was the last phrase that was played, and what was the last note of the last phrase that was played, and what should follow that?

Two: What music has been played throughout the history of jazz that has to be avoided, leaving me only what's left as material for the next phrase?

Three: Where would I like to get to by the time my playing is finished?

All that in a split second during a pause in my phrasing.

In September 1953, the phone rang. It was Charles Mingus. "Paul, you've got to help me out, I need a conductor for an orchestra." He'd written some quite complex music and he felt that he wasn't up to conducting it. And by the way, he added, would I also do a trio date with him and Art Blakey?

My only questions were where, and when.

Both dates were for Mingus' own label, Debut Records. The large group was for a singer, Janet Thurlow, and a ten-piece orchestra including Mingus on bass, Kenny Clarke on drums, John Lewis on piano, Ernie Royal on trumpet, Danny Bank on baritone sax, Willy Dennis on trombone, Eddie Caine on alto sax and flute, Teo Macero on tenor sax, and Jackson Wiley on cello. Spaulding Givens was the arranger and I conducted.

A month later I did my piano date with Mingus and Blakey. I knew Art Blakey's style. After listening to him for years on Monday nights at Birdland I knew that he'd start quietly, then steadily increase in volume and I'd be wiped out.

The date was scheduled for 10 a.m. Of course, for jazz musicians, that's extremely early in the day. Art came in with some band boy carrying his drums and set up. He was so sleepy that he played very quietly, keeping beautiful time. That was a hell of a phone call.

When you come to New York there are certain customs and protocols. It's a tradition that for the first twelve months you're seen and not heard. You attend all the events, you make friends, but essentially it's considered gauche to expect anyone to hire you just because you're the hot flash from out-of-town, so you do a great deal of listening.

It took me about three years of listening before I felt really ready to jump on a lot of these bandstands. There were so many wonderful players around New York and I'd hire some and some would hire me. It wasn't hard finding things to learn. Everyone I was able to play with had something to teach me.

Almost all my work in the 1950s was done in black clubs in black neighborhoods. In fact, at first I didn't even play very much

Bley's first and last conducting gig with the Charles
Mingus Band. (left to right) Charles Mingus, Teo Macero, ?,
Eddie Caine, and Ernie Royal.

Paul Bley and Jackie McLean at the Copa City Club on
Long Island, with Al Levitt (drums) and Doug
Watkins (bass).

in Manhattan. I was more likely to play in Brooklyn or Long Island. We would play out in Hempstead, Long Island in a black private after-hours club where someone would greet you at the door and if they didn't know you, you didn't get in. There wasn't a cover charge, it was just a private club. The success of those gigs, of course, depended on the drummer. If you had a drummer that could swing, it didn't matter what anybody else did. You could stretch out or stretch in and no one cared. If you showed up with a drummer that couldn't swing, they'd throw you out the door. A great drummer paid the rent.

I got a quintet gig at the Copa City in St. Albans, Long Island which lasted for months. I hired Jackie McLean, Donald Byrd, Arthur Taylor, and Doug Watkins. These guys all loved each other and knew each other's moves and to drive with them in the car was hilarious. They were like a bunch of porpoises, always roughing each other up and laughing, a real band—I was the outsider. For me it was an incredible education—I comped for six weeks while I found out what they were doing.

Then there was the Bucket of Blood in Mount Vernon, New York, where we had a very enthusiastic audience. At 1:00 a.m. when the band finished, they made a circle around the bandstand and said, "You ain't going anywhere. If you quit now there's gonna be a riot." We were a hot band, and we knew that with an audience like that, in a place with a name like the Bucket of Blood, there was nothing left to do but keep playing.

During this period I had a manager, Monte Kay, who also managed the Modern Jazz Quartet. He introduced me to the Shaw Agency. In the fifties, the Shaw Agency booked Louis Armstrong, Dizzy Gillespie, and a lot of other people. Because of this, I had some really nice experiences. At this time they hired my trio to join Lester Young on a variety of gigs. Monte got me billing. The ads would say: "Lester Young with the Paul Bley Trio." The first gig was at the Theatrical Grill in Cleveland. I arrived early with my trio, then Prez came into the hall and unpacked, looking just like the Prez we all knew from photos and record jackets, with the porkpie hat. I was proud of him, for matching his reputation in his appear-ance, his demeanor. As everyone knows, he was a man of few words, but those few words were all short poems.

We began playing the first tune. The bar was crowded, and the bell of his horn was literally a foot or two away from my ear. The first thing that occurred to me was I had never heard anybody play with this kind of a sound before, and why not? I'd played with dozens and dozens of saxophonists. Here was a sound that had nothing to do with any other sound I'd ever heard on a horn. It was totally unlike the recorded sound, because of course "high fidelity" is a misnomer. High fidelity is merely a paper cone vibrating. *This* was high fidelity and everything else was no fidelity at all. In person, the sound was a different order of magnitude from anything you could possibly imagine on a record. It was incredibly gorgeous and expressive, it was one foot away from my ear, and we were going to be there for a week!

The second thing I said to myself was: Why doesn't everybody play this well? Here it is—why can't everybody else do it? Why is there only one person on the planet who can play with this kind of beauty, when Prez has been out here playing for decades? It should be common currency by now.

We played the week and we went on to other jobs. Finally there was a blizzard in New Jersey and Prez was an hour late for the opening night. We were getting worried, when in he strolled with snow on top of his porkpie hat, unpacked the horn for the second set instead of the first, and we asked him, Prez, how did you manage? Did you have trouble in the storm? Is your car okay? All he had to say was: "Slippin' and slidin'." Three words were one word more than he would have preferred to use.

With Lester Young at the Loop Lounge, Cleveland.
Photo by James A. Joyce.

On the road with Lester Young.

In addition to booking my rhythm sections for Lester Young, the Shaw Agency booked us with Roy Eldridge, Bill Harris, and Ben Webster as well. Working out of New York, I would take a trio to Baltimore for a week or two, with or without a horn player. I also worked with Carmen McRae at the Club Tijuana in Baltimore.

On March 17th 1954 I began a one-month engagement opposite the Louis Armstrong Sextet at Basin Street East in New York. The dressing room between sets was a place where Louis greeted his fans, who were allowed a three-minute visit while Louis sat shirtless with a towel around his neck. The ritual was always the same. The fan or musician would profess undying adulation and Louis would validate their existence by telling them to "keep on keeping on." One night I was bold enough to ask the club owner why he chose my trio to be on the same bill with Louis. His response was, "We needed somebody to clear the club between sets." In those days Armstrong made so much money for the club in four weeks that the Shaw Agency could put anyone else they wanted in the club for the other eleven months.

Once I had an offer to bring a band into a hall, but because it was a large hall it had a union minimum. You had to have at least eleven players. So I hired everybody in the Lennie Tristano school except Lennie, including all of his second- and third-level players. The day before the gig I was still one player short of the union minimum, and I met someone in the hall at Juilliard who just happened to be carrying an instrument case. I said, "Look. I've got to have a musician for tomorrow, would you please come?"

"Sure."

"Great." I told him the time and place. "What's in the case?"

"It's a ukulele."

The next day, the band filed into the hall, we played all the standards à la Lennie Tristano, without the original melody. The ukulele player knew all the tunes so he kept playing the melody on every tune, although he asked me if I wanted him to continue playing in the second chorus. I said, "No, the first chorus is fine." The most important thing was that I had someone sitting in the chair.

None of the Lennie Tristano players, when I went to pay them at the end of the night, mentioned the fact that there was a ukulele player on the job. This was the true birth of the cool.

Lee Konitz and Paul Bley frequented the jam sessions
held regularly at Lennie Tristano's studio.
Photo by Jean-Pierre Leloir.

4

Road to L.A. – Baker

In spring of 1954, I signed a contract with Mercury Wing Records for my trio with Al Levitt, drums, and either Peter Ind or Percy Heath, bass. My next record date as a pianist was recorded in New York City and released in July of 1954.

At the time, Al Levitt was my roommate. I remember one cold winter evening in 1955, a phone call came from out of the blue and a voice at the other end of the phone said, "Hello. This is Chet Baker. Would you like to come out and join my quintet at Jazz City in Hollywood for a month starting March 9?"

I thanked him profusely for offering me the opportunity to leave the snow behind and visit L.A. for the first time. Al looked pretty despondent when he heard the news. I said, "Don't worry, Al, we'll go out there together and when the month is up we'll gig."

Chet was the James Dean of jazz. He looked like Dean. He drove fast convertibles like Dean, and young women lined up to see him. His band, which included Phil Urso, tenor sax, and Peter Littman, drums, were all very badly hooked junkies. Chet had just achieved worldwide notoriety for his work with the piano-less quartet with Gerry Mulligan.

During intermission, Chet would sometimes invite me to take a ride in his red European convertible. Like Dean, he raced sports cars, which still did not prepare me for the way he drove. He didn't drive on streets, he drove in alleys, sidewalks, and various shortcuts. When Chet drove, people were safe on the streets.

When the month was over, as I had promised, alto saxophonist Charlie Mariano invited me and Al to play with him in Palm Springs. Charlie suggested that we buy two fifteen-dollar cars so that in case one of them broke down we could all pile into the other. I noticed that it was a risky proposition, because when I looked down at the floorboard I could see the white line on the highway. As he predicted, a loud noise from the engine preceded the abandonment of one of the vehicles en route.

Later that spring, I toured with singer Dakota Staton, preceding Art Tatum, Erroll Garner, and Marian McPartland at the Town Tavern in Toronto. In the summer of 1956, I came back from one of these trips feeling pretty good and walked into Birdland. There, near the door at the back where I usually stood, was this tall, very skinny cigarette girl, wearing a short skirt, carrying a tray with a strap around her neck, looking very uncomfortable. The way I was feeling, it was clearly my duty to talk to her. After all, I didn't have a care in the world, so why should she?

"So, what's the problem?"

I shouldn't really have asked, because the list was very long: she had just started on this job, she was being pinched by the owner, etc., etc. Her name was Karen Borg.

I said, "Well, it's really very simple. You put your tray down, and you walk out the door and you proceed with your life."

She put the tray down, and we walked out the door.

It was very hot weather and the next day we took the subway to Coney Island for a swim. Karen, who preferred to be called Carla, was very much an earth person from California. She didn't

Washington, July 1956.

Paul Bley

Jazz Is Just About Ready For Another Revolution, Says Canada's Young Pianist

By Bob Fulford

JAZZ IS JUST about ready to soar off into yet another new world in a 1950s revolution that may be as radical as that of the early '40s. That summarizes the opinion of Paul Bley, the 22-year-old Canadian whose piano playing is beginning to fascinate jazz fans.

Bley, in Toronto for a date at the Town tavern, said he thinks jazz is now coming close to the end of its postbop period of assimilation. It's ready for a new revolution.

"RIGHT NOW," he said, "everybody is trying to take in all the past schools of jazz. I think most of the young jazzmen today are listening hard to the schools of the past. They're trying to select the best features of each of them and assimilate them into their own playing. For instance, I have tapes of records by Louis, Roy, Blanton, Christian, Lester, and a lot of others. We carry them around with us and play them whenever we get the chance.

"I think a lot of other musicians are doing the same thing. It's a natural cycle, the cycle that's evident in the history of classical music over the last 500 years. First a period of radical change, when all the leaders and their followers reject everything that's gone before—just as in the bop days. Then a long period of assimilation, followed by another great change."

How will the change come? Bley doesn't know, but he does have some idea what roads he wants to travel.

"AFTER LISTENING to so much old jazz during the past year, I think I'm finally able to put to use some of what I learned about composition in the years at Juilliard. I think I understand my medium a lot better.

"Now I'm anxious to do some writing. I'd like to write in longer forms, of course—62-bar compositions, perhaps. I'd like to work with superimposed harmonics and try to write music without a chordal center. I'm also interested in using the pre-Bach forms—the type of thing that 20th century composers are beginning to discover only now."

A listener had heard Bley last year and thought his playing stilted. Now it seemed to swing easily with a pleasant grace. Did Paul think he was swinging more than a year ago? "I think everybody is," he said.

AS THIS IS written, he's working jazz clubs with drummer Al Levitt and bassist Jimmy Corbet. He has various plans—for a European trip, for a return to California, for a possible jazz workshop, and for some record dates. Eventually, though, he hopes to settle in Toronto and Montreal, making frequent trips to the United States.

But wherever he goes he's likely to be marked as a young jazzman with a difference—if for no other reason than for the answer he gives when he's asked his main influence. He answers with two words and a smile. The words: "Louis Armstrong."

Paul Bley

July 13, 1955

Down Beat, July 13, 1955.
Courtesy of *Down Beat* magazine.

48

have a bathing suit so she took two scarves and made some kind of top for herself and we went swimming. The scarves must have been of a color that, unknown to me, was irresistible, and our relationship wasn't the same after that.

I knew nothing about her, certainly not that she had anything to do with music, although the fact that she was working at Birdland should have been a clue. As it happened, her father was a Swedish piano teacher who lived in the woods in California. Carla told me how her mother had died in her arms, and how she found herself living on the beach before it was fashionable. She had come east on an odyssey with her boyfriend, who took her home to his Mom. Mom was totally upset and threw her out. She worked her way to New York and found herself in Birdland. All this I found out over a time. Eventually she showed me some photos of herself as an entertainer in a Navy club in San Diego, playing piano and singing.

In October 1956, Monte Kay, who later married Diahann Carroll, offered me a university tour of the Midwest. Three weeks with a trio: Lennie McBrowne on drums and Hal Gaylor playing five-string bass. The trio agreed to use the tour as a springboard for going on to Los Angeles.

I was the leader. Nowadays it's very unfashionable for somebody to be a leader. We do everything to create the impression that there is no leader. But in those days, especially when a band was traveling, there was definitely a "leader," who was supposed to be a father figure to the band. The rest of the band were the children in the leader's family. There were leaders who could get work and leaders who couldn't get work. I was a leader who *could* get work, although that's an impulse of mine I've always fought against. Any time the organization was successful, or I was successful because of my abilities to get work, I'd make sure I'd spend a long time not trying to get work. Having gone from somebody who couldn't play at all to somebody who could play a little, to somebody who could play well enough to get hired by other musicians, to somebody who changed the prevailing style, and then somebody who put that style back into the sideman market just to check it again, I'm always on the alert as to whether the music itself has the power, or whether it all has to do with my own ambition. At one point in New York, I sold my car to make sure I wouldn't get hired for gigs just because I could get the band to New Jersey.

As for the audience, they prefer the band to have a leader. They want to be in somebody's power.

In the course of this tour, playing in a narrow belt from Texas up to North Dakota to all these weird university town captive audiences, we were offered a job in Juarez, Mexico. We discussed it, and decided to take the job, which was to last a month or two, because it would get us closer to Los Angeles. We drove to Juarez, and when we got there we found out the place was this huge club, and outside was a big yellow neon sign flashing on and off that said PAUL BLEY TRIO in script. We said, "My God, yellow neon, this means months!"

We played the first night, went back to the newest motel in Juarez and I found a giant furry brown tarantula in the shower. It was the size of my hand. After getting it out of the motel, I went to bed and woke up the next morning out on the front lawn. There had been a small leak in the rubber tubing of the gas heater and somebody had found me passed out. Two attempts on my life and I hadn't been there 24 hours.

On Saturday, the government changed and we got fired. The club didn't exist after that. On Sunday, we drove out of town for the final time, and in the rear-view mirror I could see the neon sign blinking PAUL BLEY TRIO. And that's how we finally got to L.A.

Midwest U.S. college tour on the way to L.A.
with Hal Gaylor, Bley, and Lennie McBrowne, 1956.

As soon as we arrived we were invited to play at a New Year's Eve party at the home of Lucille Ball and Desi Arnez in Palm Springs. As was the fashion at the time, they lived in a very fancy bungalow on a tennis court at the Palm Springs Country Club, and that's where we played their party.

On the road, we would finish playing and, because it was easier to travel at night, get in the car and drive to the next gig. Instead of sleeping and eating, I was living on Pepsi-Cola at seven in the morning. An hour before midnight at Lucy and Desi's, I fell back from the piano and collapsed on the floor. Lucy rushed over and said, "What's wrong?" I explained that it was nothing, I was just having a little distress from being on the road.

"Just let me rest," I said, "and I'll be okay."

"No," she said, "I want you to go to the hospital, as my guest."

At the Palm Springs Hospital they diagnosed internal bleeding. They didn't let me leave for a week. If I had followed my better judgment, which was to take a five-minute break then finish the gig, I would have been dead. Lucy was an incredible lady, the opposite of a star, completely maternal and I can honestly say I owe her my life.

I stayed in the Palm Springs Hospital and had intensive tests. Apparently there was a dot the size of a pencil mark on my stomach lining, and nobody could be sure what it was—but I had all the symptoms of an ulcer, so I was treated for a duodenal ulcer.

I've rarely had a hotel room that was as nice as this Palm Springs hospital. Room service, purple sunsets on the desert, and Lucy picked up the tab. Then I went to the Scripps Institute in La Jolla for more tests. It was even fancier than the Palm Springs hospital.

I was having a great time, when I should have been afraid for my life. I said the usual thing during the examination: "Well Doc, will I make it?" Of course, I was joking. But the specialist weighed this question very carefully and then said, in this grave voice, "Well,

STARRED NIGHTLY

at the

Penthouse

MONTREAL'S OWN

★ **PAUL**
"BUZZY" BLEY

CANADA'S CELEBRATED PIANIST
AND RECORDING STAR

plus . . . SULTRY SONGSTRESS

★ **KAREN BORG**

THE   IN THE PENTHOUSE . . . ATOP

Windsor **STEAK HOUSE**

"Where the Food Is Consistently Good"

1194 Peel Street   UNiversity 6-7766

Bley's first gig with Carla Bley (Karen Borg) at Montreal's
Windsor Steak House.

we haven't got all the test results yet . . ."

Ulcers are usually attributed to three factors: diet, rest, and emotional state. The diet was lousy on tour, there was no rest, and as for the emotional state, the ulcer revealed that I had a problem. Years before, when I had first learned I was adopted, the news had sent me racing to get things done. Where I had been previously moving at the rate of a child, I began going like a bullet, as if the music itself would fill in for the lack of family, the lack of history, the lack of background, that I thought I suffered from. For years I had made it work for me, but after the stresses of life on the road, I couldn't handle it.

When they finally released me it was one of the turning points of my life. I walked out through the garden of the hospital, and I realized just to be mobile, to be able to move, was all the reward you needed in life, and that any other kind of reward was illusion. Suddenly my own career seemed unimportant. I started to become much more interested in contributing to the welfare of the jazz art form itself.

At the time, I liked Los Angeles a lot. There were palm trees, the fragrance of flowers in the evenings, pollution wasn't as bad as it became later. Carla had come out from New York to join me. She got the idea that she wanted to get married. I thought that the one thing at the bottom of every musician's priority list is marriage, so I said, "The only way I'm going to be able to decide is if we split for a little bit so I can think about it."

Carla didn't expect that, but she reacted by going up to San Francisco and moving in with an artist—a very radical guy too, as I recall. I sat home and thought about marriage, and after about a week I decided I was all for it. I caught a plane right away.

I was very elated, talking to everyone on the plane—I was going to San Francisco to get married! I went to the artist's place, knocked on the door and called Carla's name: "Here I am!"

Carla opened the door and just looked at me, as if to say, "Who's this? What's your name, fella?"

I called the guy she was living with outside. I said to him, "Look, I've come here to marry Carla. Are you ready to take that step?" He admitted that he wasn't, so I called Carla out.

"Look, I've made up my mind. I'm ready to get married."

"Oh, really?" Carla said. She looked over at the artist, who just stood there looking at the two of us, not saying a word. She said that from her point of view, marriage didn't look really very opportune at this particular time.

I said, "Well, you know my number if you change your mind. Give me a call."

Several weeks later, back in Los Angeles, the phone rang. It was Carla announcing that she was coming home. We went to Sausalito, where her father joined us. It was a church wedding, and we had a reception afterwards with rack of lamb. It was a blissful time.

Karen Borg (later Carla Bley) and Paul
at The Cellar in Vancouver, autumn 1957.

5

The Hillcrest Club

JAZZ WAS STILL LOCKED in this conundrum of atonality, where the composers were making suggestions to the players, but not necessarily getting results. Here I was in L.A. in a more close-knit environment, with less competition. In New York, there were always twenty people you could call on any instrument—in L.A. there were two. All the best players—Mingus, Dexter Gordon, and so on, had left. After years of gaining input from the scene in New York, I was in a place where the other players needed my input. Instead of listening to music and talking about it and worrying about what was best for it, I could simply go out and work every night until I found a solution.

In January 1957, as soon as I got out of the hospital I started getting work for the trio. Although some people who had lived in LA for a number of years complained about not enough work, my talents in this area had led me to compile—before I'd even left for Los Angeles—the names and addresses of forty places that had used jazz over the past two or three years. Phone call number eighteen produced the first job. After that, I began performing six nights a week, every week. I kept up that pace for two years and, having done it then, I've never felt the need to do it again. Phone call number 32 produced a six-night-a-week job at the Hillcrest Club.

The Hillcrest was on Washington Boulevard, right in the middle of the black section of Los Angeles. It was a neighborhood with a rich tradition of live performance. For us, it was a period of experimentation. Hal Gaylor, Lennie McBrowne, and I played trio for the first month, then in April we added a vibraphonist, Dave Pike, who was very well known in the community.

Usually, at least once in a decade, I had a situation where, by sheer happenstance, the material of the band and the awareness level of the audience matched, and there would be a great flurry of activity for a couple of months. That band was one of those situations. The quartet made a television broadcast on August 26, 1957, for KABC-TV as part of the "Stars of Jazz" series. We played for two years at the Hillcrest, and outside of Los Angeles we found clubs that would put a band in for two or four weeks. We went to Denver and Vancouver. We went up to San Francisco to play the Keystone Korner. Wherever we played we'd get invited back. We had a name and an audience—we could fill a club on a Tuesday night.

Back in the summer of 1955 critic Bob Fulford had called me for an interview for *Down Beat* magazine. In the July 13th issue that year, a full-page interview with me was published with the headline, "Jazz Is Just About Ready For Another Revolution." I was quoted as saying, "I am anxious to do some writing. I'd like to write in longer forms, I'd like to work with superimposed harmonies and try to write music without a chordal center." This article was deemed prescient enough for *Down Beat* to reprint it in their 50th anniversary issue, July 1994.

In an article in Vancouver's *The Province* on October 12, 1957, I was quoted as saying: "We've reached the end of the Renaissance period, during which people have been interested in all types of jazz. One day a person will come along with a horn or a piano under his arm and the revolution will have started." The writer proceeded to say, "A revolution is coming in jazz', says pianist Paul Bley, but he's too modest to say that he's preparing the way for it."

So in the fall of 1957, I thought I'd move ahead a little faster musically if I brought Herbie Spanier in on trumpet. I'd met Herbie in Montreal and had invited him down for some jobs in New York. I took a break from the Dave Pike band and sent Herbie the fare to fly down from Montreal. We played long improvised suites for trumpet and piano for a month in Beverly Hills, at Gene Norman's Crescendo Club on Sunset Strip overlooking Los Angeles. The music was completely free, without tempo, without harmony, without written composition.

Coming from Juilliard, I was able to tape a performance and look at the music very carefully. I'd find out what was promising and what wasn't, which leads to follow, and which leads to drop. Playing suites with Herbie Spanier, I realized that the problem was that we hadn't thought about what the rhythm section would be doing —we could do free music without a rhythm section, but we couldn't do it with a rhythm section. I still love Herbie Spanier. To me Herbie represents the side of humanity that I'm most interested in: the original side. I think every leader I've worked with has been an original. And I've made a study of how they handle this trait of having an original point of view, how they make it work for them.

As for myself, I was always testing my abilities against the night's work. A player coming up in the music is in a situation where you're trying to learn how to play, where you're forced to do more than you're able to do. The ideal climate for you is the least ideal climate for the rest of the players. They can play, you can't. You can't get better unless you play with them. Yet why would they play with you if you can't? Those are the givens in every situation when you're trying to learn how to play.

At first, as a young player, whenever I ran into those challenges, the bands I played with forced me to get it together very quickly—

KLAC–TV program, Los Angeles, 1957. Paul Bley (piano), Dave Pike (vibes), Charlie Haden (bass), and Lennie McBrowne (drums).

PASADENA, CAL. SATURDAY, APRIL 27, 1957

THE JAZZ LAB

Bley's Quartet May Be '57's Best

Bley, Pike, Haden and McBrown; It's jazz.

By GEORGE LAINE

Paul Bley has impact.

And so do the rest of the members of the Paul Bley and the newly-organized quartet, now in action at Zucca's Cottage.

The membership of this tight little fraternity includes Lennie McBrown at the drums, Charles Haden at the bass and the newest addition—Dave Pike late of the Jazz Couriers at the vibes.

In New York, Lee Mortimer attested that Paul did a "bang up job." In Variety, a staff writer said that Bley possessed "drive and enthusiasm." Met romance's Bill Coss lauded Paul's "quiet aggressiveness" and Robert Sylvester, in the Daily News said that Paul was "fine, new and modern."

I'd like to get on that band wagon. Bley swings hard or soft depending on the tune. He never lets down complete, however and that's the secret of Paul's king sized success.

At Zucca's Paul felt that he couldn't properly fill the room with trio only. He sought out Dave Pike to fill in on vibes—a success.

I'm pretty enthused about the sound of the Paul Bley Quartet. It's the same instrumentation the Modern Jazz Quartet uses, the same that Cal Tjader uses in his quartet. But the sound presentations. The sound is vastly different and I guess that this is Bley's fault. In short, the quartet swings. Hard.

Even on the ballads, there is a sort of leashed power that is straining to be free. It's a tremendous thing to watch unfold in a room like Zucca's. Even the patrons at that establishment seem to be caught up in the feeling Bley achieves.

I'm tabbing Paul Bley's Quartet as the best new jazz group of 1957—if they can stick together.

Lately, that's been a chore for even the established jazz combos.

July 25, 1957

Paul Bley Quartet

Personnel: Paul Bley, piano; Dave Pike, vibes; Charlie Hayden, bass; Lennie McBrown, drums.

Reviewed: Second week of six week minimum engagement at the Hillcrest Club, Los Angeles, Calif.

Musical Evaluation: This new group led by the 24-year-old Canadian pianist concentrates principally on two lines of musical approach; playing as many as possible of their own originals, discarding a standard for every new composition reworked, and displaying a bassist's conception that self-dom lets up.

There is a high degree of original thought evident in the musical efforts. From a medium tempo'd *Both Worlds*, which offers and leaves on a vibes and cymbal sound, Bley may follow with an assortment of his own a-

Two reviews of the Paul Bley Quartet (Charlie Haden, Dave Pike, and Lennie McBrowne) when they appeared at the Hillcrest Club, Los Angeles, in April and July, 1957.

in fact, by the next set. But once I had learned the genres, and played the repertoires of the different bands, it was time to move on. Because in none of those genres was the music coming together the way that I felt it could. I was mastering all the *parts* of the music—they were no problem. The problem was defining an approach that would bring them all together—tempo and non-tempo, atonality and tonality, written and improvised—in a new and profound way.

Herbie Spanier and I sounded great as a duo, but it didn't work at all with a rhythm section. In retrospect, the reason is obvious. We were seven years ahead of our time. We had jumped into totally free playing. There had to be a period of playing free, with time, before we could play totally free. Totally open music didn't arrive until years later, when Albert Ayler formed his quartet with Don Cherry, Gary Peacock, and Sunny Murray.

I returned to the band at the Hillcrest with the problem unsolved. As hard as Herbie and I worked to put all these elements together, and as hard as the Third Stream composers were trying to put it together, we were all waiting for something, we knew not what. Unknown to us, we were waiting for Ornette Coleman to join our band at the Hillcrest Club.

6

Coleman – Cherry – Haden

IT HAS ALWAYS BEEN my practice that when a player would leave the rhythm section, I would invite him to bring in his own replacements. I figured that the players were the ones who had to get "married," so they might as well choose. Similarly, if one of the players in the band tells me about somebody he would like to have sit in, then for sure he can sit in. After all, I'm paying him for his judgment, so how can I question his choice of a guest? But during the week at the Hillcrest Club, there was a policy of no sitting in. This wasn't the management's policy, it was our idea. We were trying to get things done, trying out new material and new approaches, so no matter who showed up to sit in, we sent them to the Monday night jam session with Les McCann.

Hal Gaylor decided to move back east. We needed a bass player, so Lennie McBrowne brought Charlie Haden to an audition. Charlie arrived barefoot. Not only was he without shoes, his choice of notes left something to be desired. But his time was impeccable, and my experience as a bandleader had taught me that although it would be easy enough to find a bassist who could get the right notes, I would be very lucky to find another bassist who could play time like that. And given the chance to work every night over a series of months, Charlie figured the harmonic problems out for himself.

After Lennie McBrowne decided to go back east to join Horace Silver, Billy Higgins joined the band and Charlie and Billy Higgins became the talk of Los Angeles. Their time was so infectious that once, at an after hours jam session I attended, they played a set of time together, unaccompanied by any horn players or pianists. It was the only time I've ever heard a rhythm section playing nothing but rhythm for a whole set without leaving you wanting anything else.

One night Billy said that a friend of his, who played trumpet, had brought a saxophone player with him and wanted to sit in. Despite our policy, because no member of my group had ever invited someone to sit in, I said "no problem." He introduced me to Ornette Coleman and Don Cherry and without ever having heard either of them play before, we began playing our first piece together as a quintet.

Several things happened almost at once. The audience en masse got up, leaving their drinks on the table and on the bar, and headed for the door. The club literally emptied as soon as the band began playing. The second thing that happened was that during the first saxophone solo, large parts of the music had no discreet notes that one could say were being played. As a pianist, all my notes are readily-identifiable parts of well-tempered scales, so on the spot I had to reassess my role in the group. Another thing that happened was that, for example, while Ornette was soloing on a 32-bar piece, suddenly he would play eight bars that had no relationship, or relatively little relationship to anything else in the piece. They were phrases that he would play because they fit in eight bars.

Don Cherry's playing contained more known material and so was more easily understood. But the real surprise was, when we played a second piece, which was a Coleman original, although the solos started in the key of the original, rather than following an AABA form, they followed an A to Z form. This I had never heard done before by anyone, not in the writing of those composers who we had hoped would lead us out of the bebop wilderness, and certainly not in front of a rhythm section that was playing time. In a single gesture, all the constraints of repetitive structure fell away. The music was very exciting, the logic of it was obvious, and as soon as I heard it I realized that from now on, this was the only way to play with a rhythm section.

Having this happen on a random night of a two-year job was a surprise, but it didn't take more than a second to understand that this was the missing link between playing totally free, without any givens, and playing bebop with changes and steady time.

After the first set was over, Carla and I went out to the parking lot to have a talk.

"If we fire Dave Pike and hire Don Cherry and Ornette Coleman, we won't last out the week. What should we do?"

We looked at each other and smiled and both said, "Fire Dave Pike."

There was a precedent for this. In all my time in New York, sitting in with bands and so forth, if another piano player tapped you on the shoulder and said, the leader says it's okay for me to sit in and you left the piano stool, if that pianist sitting in played better than you, you *really* left the piano stool. Suddenly you were a member of the audience, he was onstage, and everybody in the club—the band, the leader, the guests sitting in—everybody understood that you were no longer a member of the band.

The next afternoon we called a rehearsal for the quintet. We played a mixture of Monk tunes, Bird tunes, my tunes, Carla's tunes and Ornette's tunes. Ornette had a very deep compositional bag, so every day we would learn a dozen tunes, none of which were constructed like any of the other tunes he wrote. So that tune number one might have steady time until the bridge, and then the bridge might be a ballad, and then the last four bars of the song would be double time and during the solos we had to play our solo against the rhythm section that was moving according to the rhythm of the written material, so there was a suite of rhythms for each chorus. That was the device for Tune One.

Tune Two would have an entirely different premise. Tune Two would be the fastest tune you could imagine—and fast I thought was a specialty of mine—but these guys played even faster, yet without tempo. The tempo only started after the tune was over and the improvisation began, and it too was extremely fast, without any chord changes.

Each tune had an entirely different premise. There were no piano parts, and all the tunes required harmonization, so there would be a part for the piano to play. I would ask Ornette what he would like the piano to do in a particular passage and he would say, "Make it up."

This was no problem, I'd been hearing "make it up" ever since my Bar Mitzvah. In any case, at the end of the rehearsal we had close to a dozen new tunes for the book, besides our normal repertoire that we now played with the quintet. We called a rehearsal for the day after the second night, and there were another dozen tunes, many of which had their own sets of procedures unlike one another. We rehearsed every day during the week, so we had five days of rehearsals with a dozen new tunes added at each session. At the end of the first week, the book had sixty tunes in it, in addition to the book that preceded it. The second week—there was no bottom to Ornette's bag! And all the music had to be in place by nine o'clock that night. If you had trouble wrestling with one of these procedures, you had to have solved the problem by nine o'clock that night, because at nine o'clock we were on.

I spent a lifetime listening to music, following the history of jazz through the part that preceded my arrival in New York and for close to a decade afterwards, and I've never come across so many

Liner for "Coleman Classics" LP (IAI 373852)
The Paul Bley Quintet, with Don Cherry, Ornette Coleman,
Charlie Haden, and Billy Higgins, at the Hillside Club,
Los Angeles, 1958.
Photos by Roberto Masotti and Ray Ross.
Collage by Carol Goss.

different ways to play in a matter of days. It was mind-boggling. But as Billie Holiday sang, "...the impossible will take a little while."

For the duration of that gig, if you were driving down Washington Boulevard past the Hillcrest Club you could always tell if the band was on the bandstand or not. If the street was full of the audience holding drinks in front of the club, the band was playing. If the audience was in the club, it was intermission.

We really thought that composition would point the way, because our jazz experience—regardless of how any of us felt about the song form—had taught us that the direction of the improvisation is described by the nature of the written material. Suddenly, it was clear that the improvisation could be directed not by the nature of the composition, but by the nature of what the *premise* is to improvise on.

From a musical point of view, it was extremely stimulating, but from a traditional bebop point of view, it was shocking, because bebop didn't use microtonality. That was one of its problems: it could see no way to go except into endless permutations of well-tempered notes. Ornette introduced the idea of erasure phrases, where there were some phrases that were tonal and well-tempered, and some phrases that were deliberately not tonal and well-tempered. This meant that, among other things, there was no way you could transcribe his solos onto paper, which led some people to question Ornette's technical ability, although in this case it was the technical limits of musical notation that were at fault, not Ornette.

If Ornette hadn't been a composer, it would have taken him a great deal longer to be accepted by the critics, and then by the musicians. In fact, when Ornette went to New York, the more erudite critics performed a yeoman service in giving him some kind of validity. They didn't only acquaint the public with the music, they acquainted a lot of musicians with the music. In fact, what the critics were saying was the only thing that gave him any chance of getting a gig, because on a one-to-one basis, everybody was very much in a hurry to dismiss him. It was a lot easier to dismiss Ornette than it was to figure out what was going on.

During the time at the Hillcrest, I had a chance to hear all these theories put into practice. I recorded every night with my own equipment, which happened to be top of the line for the time: a mono Ampex 600 reel-to-reel tape recorder and some very good RCA 77D microphones—the equivalent of professional studio equipment, set up on a table right next to the piano. Not enough microphones, so that the piano was low in the mix, but we recorded everything for the whole gig. There's more information on my recording of the horns than there is on Ornette's Atlantic records, where the sound of the band is flattened out and equalized. The band was never equal. The sound of the band was alto *way* on top. Equalizing it, because the sound engineer thought it would be a nice idea, was the wrong perspective.

The owner of the Hillcrest—a very nice Jamaican guy—just did not understand what had happened. He was in denial. This band had done so well for him. Three of its original members were still on the bandstand. The customers were the same, the band was almost the same, and he just couldn't understand what happened. It took him a month to realize that he could no longer afford having an atom bomb go off in his club every night. With much regret, he told us that he had to let us go. But by that time, there was a month of tape under my belt to review, with dozens of procedures that I'd never been exposed to previously, and I was ready to be at liberty again.

I headed down the road looking for opportunities to sit in, to see how all this related to music in California in 1958. At Howard Rumsey's Lighthouse Cafe I sat in with a classic Bob Cooper-type

L.A. band. I pulled out all the stops, and they offered me the job on the spot, which I refused. I went to two or three other clubs: they loved my playing and offered me the job. Shelly Manne, all kinds of people, were offering me work.

I took all these job offers as a personal slight. If I'd learned as much as I thought I had at the Hillcrest, why did all these bebop players want to hire me? So I decided to book another band of my own, just up the street from the Hillcrest at a club that later became famous, the "It Club." I went in there with Scott LaFaro on bass, Bobby Hutcherson on vibes, and Larance Marable on drums. Scotty was so amazing that we put the bass at the front of the bandstand, so you had to crane your neck to see the vibraphonist and the pianist. That was the first time a bass player had stood in front of a group for a long, long time. Maybe Ellington put a bass player up front once a week. But Scotty deserved the front chair— he was the best player in the band and make no mistake, there *is* a best player in any band, a second-best player, a third-best player and so on. With this band, no matter who you were, if you came in that club and sat down and heard the bass player playing all the charts, no matter how complicated they were, he would have your attention. The gig at the It Club was a six-month contract, but after a few weeks Carla and I kept hearing about the final season of the School of Jazz, in Lenox, Massachusetts.

It was a summer jazz school that John Lewis had founded. This would be its final year, and Jimmy Giuffre, Charles Mingus, George Russell, Ran Blake—all kinds of people—would be there.

I was beginning to feel that I had no choice but to take this music to New York and see if it would float. Finally, Carla and I decided that we had to be at Lenox. I sold my tape collection for the price of the blank tape. The guy was very concerned. "Look, I'm just paying for the blank tape. These tapes are all full of music. Shouldn't it be extra?"

I said, "No, I'm traveling light." I got rid of everything—including some stuff with LaFaro, Hutcherson, and Cherry that I regret—except for the most recent sessions at the Hillcrest. We packed up all our things, stopped by the It Club to tell the band goodbye, and drove out of town.

Thirty years later, I met Bobby Hutcherson at the Antibes Festival in southern France. He said, "What happened, Paul? Your name was out in front, you came by the bandstand and said good night, and left us without a leader!"

We drove nonstop for three days, and got to Lenox at eleven at night. We ran down the hill to hear them announce that this would be the final tune of the final set of the final night of the Lenox School of Jazz. Ran Blake was sitting at the piano and every musician at the school was there. I tapped Ran on the shoulder and said, "Hi, Ran. Can I sit in?"

Ran is a man of generous instincts. So I got to play the final tune with the all-star band. This was my first chance to check out the playing on the East Coast and see how it had progressed, and if I could relate what I'd learned.

I had one tune to play and I played like my life depended on it. The next four years of employment all derived from that one tune. Jimmy Giuffre, George Russell—I was re-invited to play with Mingus. Everything but the Sonny Rollins job came out of that set.

John Lewis woke up the next morning and found me and Carla sleeping under his piano. We got up from the floor, said our goodbyes, and headed for New York. We had made it just in time. If one traffic light had been red instead of green at one intersection across the country it would have been too late.

7

Russell – Evans – Giuffre

WHEN CARLA AND I ARRIVED in New York from Lenox, it was my plan to see who would hire me, and bring my new revolutionary ideas about playing the piano into the mainstream of jazz. It was one thing for everybody to tell me these were good ideas; it was another thing for them to give me a job. Remember, these ideas came out of working with Ornette Coleman and Don Cherry— horn players who played many notes that had nothing to do with pitch. In jazz there was always a blue note—a flatted third, a flatted fifth, a flatted seventh, or a double flatted note, but this was the extent of microtonality in jazz prior to 1957.

How the piano dealt with this situation was completely up to me. Having never been a lover of chords—I always thought that a chord was a vertical melody played simultaneously—if a chord couldn't be stripped down and each note made to line up to make a meaningful melody, it wasn't a good chord. This was not the normal procedure of playing chord changes. The normal thing was to find a style and play that style throughout all your music, altering a few notes from time to time depending which decade you were in.

When I got to New York, people would stop me on the street and say, we know you've done some playing with Ornette and Don—what is it they're doing? They hadn't even gotten to the

Five Spot yet, but there was already advance word about what was happening. This was one of the three times in my life that I possessed information that nobody on the planet had as a keyboard player. I was unique in having to deal with translating that music. Up until quite recently, when Geri Allen joined Ornette's quartet, I believe the keyboard had not really been tested in the context of his music.

Having a piece of information that no one else on the planet has is very exciting, but in retrospect it can be dangerous, and my motto now is I would prefer to be second or third rather than be first. First is the hard way.

A year or so after I got back to New York, 1960 to be exact, there was a phone call from George Russell inviting me to be part of a project he was doing for Decca Records. It was a piece for two pianos and orchestra, which involved a lot of written music. There was one condition. A large orchestral score went with the gig, and if I'd come over he'd give me the score. I'd have thirty days to practice it and return it to his apartment, at which time I would play the score. If I made a single mistake, the assignment would be given to another pianist.

I took the score home and went into the music room and Carla put trays of food under the door for the next thirty days. When I went back to his apartment there was no question of whether I would make a mistake. I hadn't just learned it, I *was* that music. I played the score without the slightest hesitation and went to the record date for Decca Records. Bill Evans was on piano A and I was on piano B.

I knew Bill socially because I'd met him when he arrived in New York, five or six years after I got there, and after working with Miles he'd become very popular on his own. In fact, by the time of this George Russell session, he was everybody's favorite pianist, and rightly so. Riverside Records had even called one of his albums *Everybody Digs Bill Evans*.

The piece called for a lot of improvising by the two pianists, in three or four lengthy non-orchestral sections, accompanied by George playing strung beads pulled over the surface of small drums, and a rhythm section playing odd time signatures, 12/8 and so forth. We started with the rhythm section playing this very off rhythm. This was my universe—rhythm sections that played wrong, no harmony or melody given. This was the atmosphere I normally breathed, and what flashed through my mind was, now, am I going to make it easy for Bill, or am I going to make it hard for Bill?

Because everybody loved Bill Evans. He already owned ninety-nine percent of the jazz piano business. And I was hoping that I could get a corner on some part of the one percent that was left. So I threw the kitchen sink at him in the first phrase—and was appalled to hear him throw it right back at me. This was good and bad news.

The whole date went that way. No matter what I did, Bill was right there tossing it back—leading, following, doing everything George could have hoped for. After the first take, as the rhythm section faded out, George rushed up and kissed us on both cheeks and said that no one had ever played his music properly before. The rest of the record date went fine. The orchestral music was read correctly, there were three or four more long two-piano-with-rhythm sections, and we all left in a blaze of glory.

The following week Bill's trio opened at the Village Vanguard. I thought, well I've spilled the beans and on Tuesday night everyone in the world will have access to my secrets. I'm going to go to the club and I'm going to hear Bill Evans play as freely and openly as he's just done on "Jazz in the Space Age." And the bit of the one percent of the jazz piano market that I thought I might have had a corner on would dry up and blow away.

Evans opened the first set with "Someday My Prince Will Come," sounding then and for the rest of the evening just like the

Bill Evans, Ron Carter, and Paul Bley.
Photo shoot at Ron Carter's apartment, New York City,
for the Japanese *Swing Journal*'s 1976 Jazz Calendar.
Photo by Mitsuhiro Sugahara.

Bill Evans that everybody loved. I was *very* relieved. I went back to the kitchen afterwards to say hello to the guys in the band.

In the kitchen, Bill asked me, "What was it we did the other day?"

I was all set to launch into a long monologue about how to play free, post-Ornette Coleman—and then I thought about Lester Young.

"Bill," I said, "we were just slippin' and slidin.'"

Later in 1960, I received a call from Ran Blake to come up and play a concert at Bard College, where he was either a student or a teacher at the time. Actually, Ran stuck around the campus for so long after he graduated that they hired him to teach. He also mentioned that a friend of his from Yale University, Steve Swallow, would like to come by and maybe sit in. Steve was an English literature student at the time. I said, "Yeah, sure, send him over."

We played the concert at Bard and spent the night in the dorm. I'd been living in New York for so long that I was startled when the birds started singing so loudly at dawn that I had to close the windows. I wasn't used to being awakened by nature.

Steve played so very well at the concert that I told him he should come to New York. I like to say that I kidnapped him, because his parents must have been very shocked. He quit Yale and came to New York and Carla and I installed him in an unoccupied loft next door to ours on Sixth Avenue. We ran wires over the fire escape and he had a light bulb, and there he was in New York. Steve and I wound up playing two years of Saturday afternoons at a coffee house with piano and upright acoustic bass. Musicians, including trumpet player Bill Dixon, would stop by on Bleecker Street and say hello.

During this period, I was hired by Jimmy Giuffre. Actually, Jim Hall hired me. I was working with Oliver Nelson at the Five Spot, opposite Giuffre with Jim Hall and Ralph Peña. Jim was leaving the band and asked if I would take his place. Giuffre was up for it, because he remembered me playing that tune at Lenox. I went over to his house and played and I got the gig. But there were two big problems. The first problem was that he didn't have a bassist. Ralph Peña was leaving to go back to the West Coast.

The second problem was getting in the way of me helping to solve the first problem. Jimmy had been so avant garde so early that he was used to the idea that nobody was going to be on his wavelength. When he was playing in Los Angeles in the fifties, he had already formulated a unique compositional style, but of course, whenever he rehearsed his pieces with jazz musicians, as soon as they finished the written music, they reverted back into their normal bebop combo pattern of playing. So Jimmy had developed the habit of writing out how he would like the players to improvise on each piece.

I said, "I have a bassist for us. But you have to promise me one thing: if I bring him by, you won't say a word to him about how you want him to play."

Jimmy agreed, but for a month I wouldn't bring Steve Swallow by. I didn't want the experience to be spoiled for him. I had to be sure, until finally Jimmy was desperate for a bass player.

"Okay," I said, "Just remember that you promised me . . ."

"Yeah, yeah, just bring him over and let's hear him!"

Steve came over and blew Giuffre's mind by doing exactly what he was hoping a bassist would do, and Jimmy kept his word. In fact, he decided to take the band to Europe. After Swallow was fully ensconced in the 1961 trio, Giuffre told us of his time in L.A. when he lived in the Hollywood Hills with a woman animal trainer. She had two large ocelots. Giuffre remembers sitting on the couch with an ocelot on each side. Finally, one day, he turned to the lady and said, "Either the ocelots go, or I do."

She chose the ocelots.

Giuffre came from Texas. He played "Texas Tenor," which involved, while walking the bar, putting the bell of the horn against the inside of his thigh, while he played for a special aural affect. A good night was when the audience would throw capped beer bottles against the wire mesh protecting the stage.

Counterpoint was the essence of Giuffre's music. His compositions were arranged so that each part could be played at whatever speed the player wanted. They only hooked up at certain points as a *tutti*. Even as a compositional idea, that was very revolutionary, but then the speed at which each player had decided to play his parts and the way that affected the musicians' relationship to one another would carry over into the improvisations, so each performance of each piece would be completely different. It's strange that Jimmy would choose to work with a pianist, because his compositional context was not harmony, but counterpoint. In my case, his contrapuntal compositional style meant that our trio acted as a quartet, because the pianist's left hand and right hand could act independently.

When Jimmy took the trio to Europe, its innovations weren't appreciated right off the bat. He was a big star at the time, having been heavily featured in the film *Jazz on a Summer's Day*, which had just come out. We landed in Frankfurt and had a big press conference at the airport, up on a dais addressing fifty or so members of the media. Then we played a concert in Vienna at the Beethovensalle, a terribly austere and imposing building.

The audience expected "The Train and the River," and here we were. At the time, Jimmy had taken to playing the clarinet without a mouthpiece. At intermission people rushed back to the dressing room, demanding "Where is Jim Hall?"

After that tour, the agency who booked us gave up the jazz concert booking business and brought the Beatles to Europe. This was in 1961. There was no avant garde in Europe—no audience,

Paul Bley, Bleecker Street, New York, 1961.
Photo by Len Dobbin.

no players, no anything. By 1965, Europe—Germany in particular—was full of free players, but in the meantime, Jimmy found himself musically triumphant, but out of work.

So the band returned to the U.S. and went back to our own projects and never dropped a stitch until thirty years later, when we reunited for a number of very successful European tours and New York club gigs. Until then, Giuffre's curse was to always be ahead of his time. The two most important figures in the early days of avant garde jazz were both composers and reed players: Ornette Coleman and Jimmy Giuffre.

After the tour with Giuffre in 1961, Steve and I resumed the Saturday afternoon duo gig at the Coffee House on Bleecker off of Seventh Avenue. One day, Atilla Zoller came by, and that's how I got my first gig in Europe as a leader. He told me to come over to a club he was playing at; there was this German radio producer there who wanted to meet me. So I went over and got the tour.

8

Rollins – Hawkins – Mingus

I WAS THE ONLY PIANIST in the world who had played with Ornette, except for a great bebop pianist on his first record, Walter Norris. Sonny Rollins was curious, Miles Davis was curious. These people didn't phone you, they sent word out through the grapevine, and sometime in 1963 the call went out. It was a Monday night, and Sonny's band and Miles' band were playing opposite each other at Birdland. The call had gone out for both Herbie Hancock and me to show up.

When I got there, Herbie said, "Hello Paul, which gig do you want?" That was very generous of him—I don't think that I would have made him the same offer.

I thought that I could be of some use to Sonny in playing what he did best: standards, but playing free on them. Sonny was in the middle of a set at the time. So I got up on the bandstand and jumped in. Sonny responded in his usual adversarial style and a marriage was born that lasted a year of touring in the U.S. and Japan and culminated in the RCA Record, *Sonny Meets Hawk.*

One of the highlights of my year with Sonny was the tour of Japan. All of us made sure our passports were in order, got packed, and made it out to the airport early. In the lounge we met the Shaw Artists Management rep, who was all in a sweat: "Where's Sonny?"

The Tokyo flight started boarding, and there was still no Sonny.

The Shaw Artists rep was shaking and pacing the floor. Here he was holding ten thousand dollars worth of tickets. This was the last flight to Japan if we were going to make the tour, and he had no Sonny Rollins. The last call came for the flight to Tokyo. The Shaw Artists rep started shouting and frothing at the mouth. Someone persuaded them to hold the door for us—without Sonny there was no point in any of us getting on the plane—and we were given sixty seconds.

Suddenly, Sonny appeared from a circular staircase. Shaved head, mohawk, carrying barbells and saxophone cases, he called out, "Let's go."

The tour was a double bill of Sonny and Betty Carter. Sonny Rollins, Roy McCurdy, Henry Grimes, and I were the rhythm section, both with Sonny and with Betty Carter. It wasn't until I was on the plane that I found out that Sonny's band was actually a quintet. It seems that Sonny had added a trumpet player from Chicago, whom I'd never heard. We sat next to each other on the plane and I was curious that he had a briefcase chained to his wrist, from which he was inseparable. So I turned to him and asked him, "What's in the case?"

He said, "It's music that I've written specially for Sonny." He was hoping that he could get Sonny to play it on the tour. I thought that since he was a new addition to the band, it was inappropriate for him to solicit Sonny, because Sonny was a great composer who had written "Oleo" and "Pent Up House" and many, many other wonderful tunes that were in wide use by musicians at the time. He didn't seem convinced.

We played the first night at Kosei Nenkin Hall at five o'clock as part of seven performances there in ten days. At the next performance on the following day at five o'clock, the trumpet player was nowhere to be found. But at a jam session at a small club after the gig, there he was sitting at the bar with the briefcase still strapped to his wrist.

I said, "Man, where were you tonight?"

I'm not in the band anymore."

"What happened?"

"I got fired."

I said, "Gee, I sure hope you've got a round-trip ticket."

From working with Charles Mingus, I already had experience with situations that required error-free transactions. It was like the military. If you survived the first day of battle, then most likely you were going to get home.

This was the tail end of an era. By the late sixties, it became more common to run a band as a cooperative, where everything was shared equally among all members even though there was usually a leader whose name and reputation had gotten the gig. That was a reaction *against* this period.

My tenure with Rollins mostly involved touring. Besides Japan, we went all over the United States, eventually landing back in Los Angeles at the It Club, just up Washington Boulevard from the Hillcrest. By this time, Sonny was playing very long pieces. He would start a tune, play for an hour and fifteen minutes, then turn to me and say, "You got it!"

That job made me very concerned with duration. At the It Club, the Saturday afternoon matinee was three hours long, then there was a four-hour evening gig.

At the beginning of the first three-hour Saturday matinee, we couldn't find Henry Grimes. We were all good friends with Henry. I had first met him back when he was playing with Marian McPartland. But he and Sonny were particularly close. Henry was a small man, with a youngish face, and Sonny was like a father to him. But Henry had been growing increasingly introverted. It was getting to the point where he would not speak unless it was absolutely necessary, and eventually he simply wouldn't speak, period.

We searched the It Club. "Has anyone seen Henry?" Finally, we looked behind the club. There was a tree in the backyard, and Henry had gone out to the backyard and climbed the tree.

Sonny tried to coax him out of the tree but got nowhere. It was time to play the matinee and Henry refused to budge. Sonny turned to me and said, "Look, could you play a little bass for me?"

I said sure, that wasn't a problem.

So he kicked off "This Can't Be Love" at a very bright tempo and played it for three hours. A long time to keep up a walking bass line on the piano. Fortunately Henry Grimes made it down from the tree for the evening session, where we played a single tune for *four* hours.

It was toward the end of my year with Rollins when the event came that Sonny had been waiting for: the record date with our quartet and one of the great tenor saxophonists of all time, Coleman Hawkins.

Sonny Meets Hawk. The record date was at the RCA Studios on 23rd Street on a Monday night, nine o'clock, so naturally enough, that's when everyone showed up. Everyone except Sonny. At ten o'clock, there was still no Sonny. At about 11:30 the call came in saying that the session would have to be Tuesday, the next night, at nine.

I had been with the band long enough to know that Sonny had no intention of showing up on Tuesday, so I gave a twenty dollar bill to the night security guard and said, "When Mr. Rollins enters the building, call me."

The call came on Friday night at nine o' clock. By that time, the rest of the band had been showing up every night and was put off each night by a phone call. When I got there they were fed up and exhausted. I walked in the door shaved, showered, and ready to play.

I'm convinced to this day that Sonny had waited a whole year until it was time to unleash those phenomenal solos on *Sonny Meets Hawk*. He was consciously holding himself back until the record date.

I don't know if Sonny knows it, but Hawkins came to me after the first tune and said, "Paul, do me a favor. For the chorus, when it's my turn to play, lead me in. Give me a nod of your head." Sonny was never where you thought he was going to be. A chorus would be ending and here would be Sonny holding an A natural, three octaves in the stratosphere for the last eleven bars, and it was up to Hawk to find his way in. So we had this little conspiracy going. Of course, once I gave him the cue, Hawkins hit as if he knew exactly what was happening and had been in total command all along.

Charles Mingus had the same kind of will power. When he called me in 1959, I immediately went to Long Island, walked up the pathway to his attached house, and climbed the stairs to his front door. Mingus greeted me warmly, then we had a thirty-minute meeting and at the end of the meeting he threw me out of his house. He would give you an incredible range of messages in a small period of time, which eventually gave him a reputation for being crazy. But I think it was a period in which he did that for openers with people, just to see how they handled both sides.

In music, that makes a lot of sense. In social situations it goes beyond most acceptable limits, but musically that kind of contrast is a good thing. Craziness is measured by whether your interactions work for you or against you. They always worked for Mingus.

There was a cocktail party he attended that was full of producers from the big record companies. In those days, they were called "A&R men"—artists and repertoire. As Mingus circulated, he would see musicians and say to them, "Well, have you asked anybody for a job?" They'd say no, that's not really what we're supposed to be here for, and he'd say, "What do you mean? There's a roomful of record executives. Ask somebody for a job."

Eventually he got into a conversation with somebody from Columbia. It wasn't antagonistic at all, but Mingus started increasing the volume of his side of the conversation. After a few minutes, he got really room-size loud. Not hostile, just loud. The executive was so intimidated by this first-time encounter that he was conceding all the points that Mingus was negotiating, hoping to get Mingus to come down in volume. The next thing we knew, Mingus was a Columbia recording artist.

Paul Bley, Sonny Rollins, Henry Grimes,
and Roy McCurdy, Japan 1963.

9

Stopping Time
Ayler – Murray – Peacock – Bley

IN 1964, CARLA AND I, and our circle of friends, which included poet Paul Haines, Steve Swallow, and later, Gary and Annette Peacock, had regular evening round-table discussions about the future of jazz, at our place on Hudson Street. We had long talks all night.

The subject was: the second revolution in jazz since 1957, the first abandoning tonality and the second abandoning time. These changes were much more all-encompassing than the difference between swing and bebop. In the 1950s, when everybody was posing temporal solutions to this problem of atonality, we all conceded that we were looking for a mainstream solution: one that could be used by the largest body of players. It was assumed that it would be necessary for as many players as possible to adopt this new *modus operandi*, whatever it would be, in order to create a new mainstream, or to take over the old mainstream. If only a few players adopted this way of playing, it would not be a mainstream, but an offshoot, a tributary that would eventually run out, leaving it as simply one of the eccentric corners of jazz. So we suffered from an overriding fear that any detour we tried might turn into a blind alley, and there were so many musical pitfalls.

Now the roles of all the instruments were up for grabs. The guitar and the piano were threatened with obsolescence, seeing as jazz was no longer a chordal-based music, but was, instead, a linear music that opened up the possibilities of a new choice of instrumental combinations.

By the 1960s, we'd already survived all the interpersonal, lifestyle type of decisions that you could ruin yourself on. Now, we were actively trying to figure out what we could play that would take us into new territory, yet still make us feel like jazz musicians, for an audience that expected jazz musicians, and for critics who expected a jazz performance. These were the criteria, all based on a traditional jazz aesthetic. We loved all of the best of the music, so we weren't trying to deny any of these musical traditions; we were trying to discover how we could add to them.

One cold February in the Village, I got a phone call from Gary Peacock. "Paul, I've got a gig at the Take 3 for two bands. You and I will play in both bands. One band will have John Gilmore and Paul Motian, and it will be followed by a band with Albert Ayler and Sunny Murray. It starts on Friday. It pays five dollars a night."

"Fine," I said. "I'll take it."

No sooner had I put the phone down than it rang again. It was Edgar Bateman, a former Miles Davis drummer.

"Paul, I'm down here in the Bahamas. I've got a jazz gig at this hotel; we have three more weeks, it's a really good quartet, but the piano player has to leave. Can you fly out Friday?"

This was the dead of winter, the job paid hundreds of dollars a week, and Edgar was a wonderful drummer. I said, "Edgar, I'm sorry. I've got a five-dollar-a-night job on Bleecker Street that I just can't say no to!"

I had the feeling that the history of jazz hinged on that five-dollar-a-night job. The ability to distinguish the important call from

Pianist–at–large in New York, circa 1964.

the unimportant call is the key to progressing in your musical development.

As it happened, that *was* a historic job. We were playing some of Carla's pieces and they all had tempo. Invariably, none of them had changes. The rehearsal was, in this case, with Sunny Murray. The piece would start off in tempo and Sunny would start playing and I'd say, "Okay Sunny, it's 1-2-3-4," counting off the time and Sunny would go "be-dah-de-dah-de-dah-de-dahdah." Playing free.

I'd say, "Sunny, this is a tune that's in time."

"No problem man, I got it!" And then the same thing would happen. So I said, "Let's try a Latin piece."

We'd kick off the tempo, and he'd play exactly the same way. We got through the first night and Carla and I went home.

Carla never stayed home when I went to the job; she always came along. She was obsessed with the music. She would play a piece for me and I would say, "Yeah, we'll play it tomorrow." She worked really hard at it. When we were both at home there was no way I could get to the piano. Carla would get up, have breakfast, and then she was at the piano. If there were guests in the house, she would be talking. Otherwise she was writing. She worked endlessly on a piece to get it just right, and that's one of the reasons her pieces sound so inevitable. Often she would be on a gig and the tunes would come out of the playing on the gig. That's what made the music so seamless. Because the playing led to the tunes, the tunes led to the playing.

So that night after the rehearsal with Sunny Murray, I said, "Carla, these tempo pieces of yours are not going to work. I can't get Sunny Murray to play in time! Tomorrow night we're going to have to play an entirely new book. We'll have to throw out all the tempo pieces and replace them with pieces without tempo."

Carla stayed up all night to rewrite the whole book. The next night we kicked off the tunes and Sunny sounded just right. With

Ornette, the bass player joined in the fray, but the drummer was *always* playing metronomic time—not necessarily four to the bar, but at least time. With the advent of Sunny Murray, Paul Motian, and Milford Graves, the drummer joined the bassist in the counterpoint. A lot of players managed to handle the absence of chord changes, although for many of them that was traumatic and still is. For myself, when the drummer gave up playing time, the music sounded totally different than it had the week before. But for a lot of musicians, not to mention a lot of listeners, the music lost *all* of its meaning.

This quartet from the Take 3 was recorded in March 1964 and later released in the 1970s as *Turning Point* on the Improvising Artists label. The quintet album *Barrage* with Marshall Allen, alto sax, Dewey Johnson, trumpet, Eddie Gomez, bass, and Milford Graves, drums, was released on ESP. Art Lange wrote in *Downbeat* August 1992: "These sessions proved a major advance on post Bill Evans piano trio interaction.... Bley relates, 'I was interested in liberating us from bar lines and chorus lengths, and in liberating the harmony of the trio and the open palate of the solo.'" Lange went on to say, "Bley's reconsideration of rhythm and harmony, form and tempo, paved the way for players as stylistically diverse as Keith Jarrett and Bill Frisell." In the sixties we saw these recordings as an explosive reaction to the absence of steady time.

10

The Jazz Composers Guild
Dixon – Rudd – Shepp – Ra

In 1964, I ran into Bill Dixon on the street in Greenwich Village. Carla and I were on Hudson Street and he lived just three blocks away, on Bank. Bill said, "We're having a meeting. Come on by."

I had a moment's hesitation. I had already had two experiences with jazz organizations, first the Montreal Jazz Workshop and then the New Jazz Society of New York, of which I eventually became president. These experiences had been successful, but of course success has always meant the end of a chapter for me. Success with anything meant that it was a good time to leave it in other peoples' hopefully capable hands.

All collectives, regardless of size, are usually run by a handful of key people who come to all the meetings and do all the work. Other people may come to the meetings, but when this nucleus breaks up, or a couple of key people leave, those other people often have no way of knowing just what has been happening all this time, and it's not always acknowledged who was really making things work.

Being one of these key people is mainly dull bureaucratic administrative work, and every time I had been through one of these situations, I vowed never to waste my time doing it again, because it isn't directly musical, it's pre-musical work. But every decade or so, somebody would make an offer. When Bill said, "Come to the meeting," I went.

What a bunch of wounded souls there were at these meetings. Talk about group therapy. It was nothing for someone to stand up at a meeting and talk for two or three hours about the pain that they felt, the struggle—inter-group, inter-race, inter-class, inter-family, inter-musical, inter-*everything*. The next night, the working nucleus of the Guild would get together and do all the work.

When I showed up, the Jazz Composers Guild had been in place for several meetings. There was already tension in the group, because of Bill's notion that we were all going to get together and form a cooperative against the record companies of the world. We would deny our services collectively to band leaders, to any record company, until we could form our own record company, which would not keep the lion's share of the profits in return for taking on minor administrative tasks, which is how the musicians perceived the record companies. However, Archie Shepp had just been offered a contract with Impulse, and Bill believed that he should turn it down. You could see his point of view; it was built into the name: guilds strike. Historically, that's what they do.

But Archie had a family to support and he sure wasn't going to turn down *any* money, certainly not a lump of money like an Impulse contract. That was it for Bill. He got up and left the meeting. He didn't return until months later. That was a problem because he was the founder.

After that, Roswell Rudd and I ran the Guild for over a year, We started putting on weekly concerts where five bands would play. By May of 1964, when the Guild produced a concert at the Cellar on West 91st Street, the Guild consisted of: the Cecil Taylor Unit, the Bill Dixon Quintet, the Paul Bley Quintet, the John Tchicai/Roswell Rudd Quartet, the Free Form Improv Ensemble

The Jazz Composers Guild, May, 1964.
(left to right) Jon Winter, Burton Greene, Bill Dixon,
Sun Ra, Paul Bley, Roswell Rudd, Carla Bley,
Mike Mantler, Cecil Taylor, John Tchicai, and
Archie Shepp.

JAZZ REVOLUTION CONTINUES

the Jazz Composers Guild presents

"4 Days in December"

at Judson Hall 165 W. 57 St., 8 PM

Dec. 28 Cecil Taylor Unit
Bill Dixon Sextet

Dec. 29 Paul Bley Quintet
J.C.G. Orchestra
works by
M. Mantler & C. Bley

Dec. 30 Archie Shepp Qrt.
Free Form Impro-
visation Ensemble
Le Sun-Ra Arkestra

Dec. 31 R. Rudd-J. Tchicai
Quartet

TICKETS FOR ALL CONCERTS
$2.50

A FEW DAYS LEFT TO PURCHASE
TICKETS AT ADVANCE SALE PRICE
OF $2 AT JAZZ RECORD CENTER,
107 W. 47 St. & SAM GOODY
RECORD SHOPS.

Village Voice, December 17, 1964.

with Burton Green, the Archie Shepp Sextet, and Le Sun-Ra Arkestra.

After the "October Revolution" Concert at The Cellar in 1964, enthusiasm was high—the phone started ringing and didn't stop ringing. We found that the New York press loved the idea of a musician-run co-op. We did concerts at Judson Hall, "Four Days in December" (December 28-31, 1964) and at The Contemporary Center, upstairs from the Vanguard (November 16, 1964, January 15 and 29, 1965, and April 9-11, 1965), which included the newly formed Jazz Composer's Orchestra Association with Carla Bley and Michael Mantler.

As it turned out, the best thing about the Guild was that it promoted all its members. The members at the time were not all equals in terms of their careers and there was a disparity in the sizes of their audiences. One night at one of our round-table discussions at home, Carla was bemoaning the fact that the Mike Mantler/Carla Bley Quintet drew small houses. A light bulb went on in my head. I had a brilliant idea, which would move her status from the bottom of the Guild's hierarchy to the top. She asked, "What's this idea?"

I replied, "It's such a good idea that I want to savor it for awhile." She followed me around the room. The secret of success of an idea is to persuade someone that he or she thought of it.

My response was, "You form an orchestra with the seven band leaders and you'll become the biggest draw."

This idea was so good that it cost me a wife.

At one point, a possibility of getting grant money for the Guild was suggested and we had a meeting with a lawyer to work out the procedure. At least a half dozen of us went to Wall Street: Sun Ra, myself, Carla, Burton, perhaps Cecil, John Tchicai, and Roswell Rudd.

The lawyer said, "Look, we have a very good chance here. I just got a lot of money for an unknown dance company and now they're buying their own building. Getting funding for an enterprise such as yours will be no problem."

Then Sun Ra got up and said, "Well, I'd like to say a few words before we get into this..." and took us to Egypt. For a brief, supposedly open-ended discussion on the origins of his present philosophy.

We were with this Wall Street lawyer in a double-breasted suit, sitting in his office with wood paneling and rows of books all over the walls. The phone rang and he took the call. While he was on the phone, Sun Ra's speech continued. When the lawyer put the phone down, Sun Ra was in the middle of saying, "...and I'm not sure we should accept this money."

For us, of course, this was a fairly normal way to begin a Guild meeting, and we were fully prepared to stay and work things out, if need be, until six in the morning. The lawyer, however, took one listen and realized that our sensibilities were far too disparate to bring together in the limited time he had to offer us. After all, Sun Ra's speech was making it clear that we had come all the way to Wall Street to refuse any chance of getting grant money.

We kept working, despite these differing philosophies and ways of offering help.

Roswell Rudd was really the counterweight to all this. The two of us did all the administrative stuff and enough got done to encourage the non-office types to show up. In general, everyone showed up every week, which in itself attested to our success, but Roswell has to be mentioned as a prime mover in getting things done.

Months later, Bill Dixon showed up at a meeting and announced that he was taking over the Guild again. We said, "Okay, no problem. We're overworked and we'd love to have you."

At this point, the meetings were very well attended, because we realized that if we stopped showing up at the meetings, the Guild would cease to exist. I was only too happy to turn this meeting over to Bill. After all, he was the founder and we had, indeed, pleaded with him to come back. As the first order of business, Bill said that he wanted the Guild's next meeting held at his house.

"Bill," I said, "It's great to have you back. But I have this feeling that if you call the meeting at your house no one will show."

At this point, we were meeting at Roswell's loft down on Hope Street. I said, "You're welcome to run the meetings, but I think we should still have them where we've been having them."

Bill said, "No. I want to have them at my house."

The meeting was called, everyone agreed to show up, and we filed out. But when the meeting time came, the following Thursday at the appointed hour, nobody showed up. I didn't show up, nobody showed up, for reasons no one knows. There were no phone calls, there was no decision in advance. And that, happily, was my final foray into the administrative side of music—at least until Improvising Artists Records, which, thank goodness, wasn't a collective project.

11

Touring Europe as a Leader

WHEN CARLA AND I BROKE UP after the founding of the Jazz Composer's Orchestra Association, it was a real tragedy for me. For one thing, it was very unexpected. She told me at three o'clock one morning that she was leaving, and she was gone by eight. It all happened in a very high and very spacey way, but it was final and irrevocable.

A week later I was sitting in my car trying to get going. The car worked fine—I just couldn't figure out where to go. My choice of directions seemed infinite. I didn't have to go home, I could head for California or Montreal or Florida if I wanted. There was nobody waiting for me any longer. Why go anywhere? For a few moments this was a real problem.

Then I realized that I had the *Closer* date to do at Columbia Records the following Thursday. An engineer friend of mine who was leaving Columbia, had offered me some 4-track studio time, so I called up Paul Haines and a few other friends and told them that I needed their presence to help me through. The rhythm section was Steve Swallow and Barry Altschul and the music was great. For better or worse, unhappy personal experiences can translate into intense musical performance.

Between May 20th and December 18th, 1965, when I recorded

Closer, I thought of a record date not as an opportunity to document music that I had been playing up to that point, but as a chance to try something that had been on my mind, to throw it out there and see if we, or anyone else, could make some sense of it. The *Closer* album consists of tapes that were made in May of 1965, at Columbia Records recording studios on the first four track recording machine ever made. In those days I rehearsed, and to expedite the rehearsal, I told the musicians to just play the written music, and only a few bars of the solo section, and then return to the final written music. So, when it came time to record, they were used to playing very short solos and we ended up with three-and-a half-minute takes.

I thought that *all* the ethnic music that had previously influenced jazz could still influence music without meter. My idea was that there should be no real radical difference just because the music was in free time and it was being made up and not written and was atonal. That didn't necessarily have to change the procedural benefits that jazz had accrued after all this time. It could still sound like a normal jazz set, there could still be a number of pieces of different character and so forth, it wasn't just a question of everybody playing as fast as possible for as long as possible. You could even play traditionally, using all the new freedoms that were available. Therefore, the albums that I made at the time, beginning with *Closer* on ESP Records with Steve Swallow and Barry Altschul, explored these other directions.

Later in the autumn of 1965, I toured Europe with Kent Carter, bass, and Barry Altschul, drums. This was the first time that I'd had a warm reception for completely free music.

A lot of credit for presenting the new music of the early sixties to the world at large goes to ESP Records. The label was owned and operated by Bernard Stollman,

This second revolution was greeted with extreme hostility by critics and the listening public; consequently, when ESP Records courageously decided to release tapes by the New York avant garde, the LPs had minimal sales. The musicians did not receive any up-front guarantees and no royalties were forthcoming. Some of the sessions, in my opinion, were as important as the Louis Armstrong Hot Fives. Sessions such as the Albert Ayler Trio with Gary Peacock and Sonny Murray and my album *Closer* epitomized the innovations of the second revolution.

Once I was at a recording session with David Izenson, Paul Motian, and Pharaoh Sanders. The phone rang. Somehow Bernard Stollman had found out that we were recording and while the playbacks were going on in the background he said, "Let me hear a little bit of it." We paused for several minutes, after which time he said, "I want it." I replied, "Bernard, you're buying a session you heard only over the telephone?"

He liked the tape more than I did. We never sold it to him.

Izenson was a fabulous character. Originally a bassist with the Pittsburgh Philharmonic, he called Ornette Coleman one day and identified himself and said that he'd come to New York to play with Ornette. After a long telephone silence, Ornette is reported to have said, "Come on over."

Later on Dave married and bought an apartment building in the East Village. As a tenant would move out of one of the apartments, he would install one of his many basses as the apartment's sole tenant. He spent his time going from apartment to apartment promiscuously visiting each of his collector's item basses.

In 1966, I had one of those dozen or so phone calls that have turned my life around. It was Annette Peacock. I hadn't seen her for years. She and Gary were separated. She was calling from Paul Haines' loft. I said, "Don't do anything. Don't leave the room, don't move. I'm coming over to get you." I ran out the door and jumped in my car. My sense of direction was no longer a problem. I headed straight over to Paul's, and by the time Annette and I left his loft together we had become mates.

Two weeks later, I had a gig in Europe and Annette came with me. It was a project that Attila Zoller had organized for Nordwestfunk Radio in Hamburg: an all-star tentet including Steve Lacy, Kent Carter, Barry Altschul, Mike, and Carla. We would all be together for four days to rehearse and record. There were usually compositions by four domestic composers and four guests, and I had commissioned pieces from both Carla and Annette.

Backstage you could cut the drama with a knife. Here were Mike Mantler and I, with two very strong-willed women, and everybody's allegiances were being stretched. It was pretty traumatic, but we got a lot of music played. Annette emerged as a composer. The music was broadcast all over Europe.

Annette had always wanted Gary to be a bandleader. He certainly qualified, as one of the best bassists in the world. But Gary had no interest in it. He was never out of work, because he was one of those rare players who you could always count on to play better than you. Like Scott LaFaro, Gary has a mean way with a phrase and the only way to understand anything about Scotty is through Gary, because they're adjacent to each other historically and aesthetically, yet represent two totally different kinds of playing. Scotty failed when it came to playing with Ornette—he played atonally, whereas Ornette played tonally, atonally, and microtonally. All he really had to do was listen, but he certainly was a complete success with Bill Evans. Peacock was a success with Albert Ayler *and* Bill Evans.

Some time after this, I was offered a month-long contract in Madrid. Annette was seven months pregnant, but elected to come along. So we went to Madrid: Annette, Barry Altschul, Mark Levinson, and I. We were there to play our only contract—four weeks at the Whiskey Jazz Club. During the last week of the gig, the Bologna Festival called: "We heard you were here. You've got to come to Bologna." I gratefully accepted.

At the end of the month in Madrid, the club owner wouldn't let us leave. In fact, he hadn't paid us for the final week yet. So the band sneaked out of town at dawn: Annette and I in an orange Volkswagen bug and Barry and Mark in another car, to drive from Madrid to Bologna.

Not having been paid, we just had enough gas money to get there. To get some nourishment, we stopped at every grapevine along the way. The trip seemed to take an awfully long time. Finally, we pulled into Bologna two nights before the gig. It was dark and raining, and we were trying to read a map and figure out the street signs, when a car screeched to a stop beside us in the middle of an intersection and a guy shouted "Paul Bley! Follow me!"

He took us to an incredible old hotel. Outside our room was a giant balcony that looked out onto the leaning tower of Bologna— a little-known wonder of the world that leans just as much as the famous one in Pisa. We'd been living on grapes for the last five or six days, so we called room service and had an incredible meal on our private balcony overlooking this spectacular structure. We had food, work, and a safe haven; and we had a baby due shortly— everything was perfect.

But I realized that this was just one festival and I now had a family to support—not just Annette and a baby on the way, but I had two Americans with me who were also my responsibility. As we were eating in the hotel room, I said, "I'm just going to have to go out there and play so well that we get a tour out of this festival."

I started preparing myself. I concentrated on the upcoming performance. We worked six months after that festival.

We had heard that Rome was a hotbed of jazz. Don Cherry, Steve Lacy, and Gato Barbieri and his wife were living in Rome.

Bley's first free band that had an audience, with
Mark Levinson (bass), and Barry Altschul (drums), 1965.

Alberto Alberti, a former bassist who was now the jazz A&R man for RCA Italiano, invited us to come to Rome and make a record date. So we drove to Rome and Alberto found us an apartment, which had some peculiarities. The apartment had bugs, thousands of them, and in the afternoon as the day warmed up, they would start to jump several inches off the floor. We bought some white powder that we were told would get rid of the bugs, and all that happened was that white bugs started jumping up and down. The apartment overlooked a monastery garden. We got up every morning to watch the nuns in their habits making their way through this charmed garden.

We had a car, and even the traffic jams always seemed to get us stuck at some spectacular fountain, or in front of a wonderful sculpture. In Italy, we had princes coming to our door. The famous Pignatelli family, who have had land holdings all through South America since the time of Columbus, had a black sheep in the family: Prince Pepito, a jazz fan and a drummer. Every night at six o'clock, Pepito and his wife Piki would pick us up in their limo and take us to restaurants, and wine bars, and jazz clubs.

On July 1, 1966, we recorded *Ramblin'* for RCA Italiano. Alberto Alberti produced the session. He opened my eyes to the Italian view of existence by explaining to me that he did not have a job at RCA, he had a *position*. In a position you travel from one mistress to another in various Italian cities for weeks at a time, only touching base at RCA in Rome to tell your superior about your adventures, and to check that the person who had the *job* was getting the job done. If all was well, you went off for another few weeks, and continued your adventurous life so that you'd have more good tales to tell your superior when you came back again.

In any case, despite all the support we were getting on every side, until we started our tour we were without funds, so when Annette went into labor she entered a convent hospital run by nuns. The baby arrived and so did the bill. We had no money to pay it. So we gave Annette and Solo Rose several days to recuperate, then I entered the hospital in the dead of night, made my way surreptitiously to their room, and opened the window to the fire escape. Annette and I carried the baby down the fire escape to the Volkswagen bug waiting below.

We also had a survival test for musicians. Since Barry Altschul was new at this game, we gave him the test. The test was that you took an American musician who spoke no foreign language and let him out of the car at noon in a capital city in Europe. To pass the test, by midnight he had to have acquired a girlfriend, a car, an apartment, something to smoke, and a telephone. If he couldn't do all that, he couldn't work in my trio.

When we hit Rome, we were in no position to take care of the two Americans with us, but Barry Altschul passed the test with flying colors. They were a rhythm section with a wide range of talents. The bassist, Mark Levinson, was so talented that later he became a well-known sound designer.

The tour that started in Rome took us to Holland, where we were drummer Stu Martin's guests on his houseboat outside of Amsterdam. We slept beside a window that opened onto the river, and we were awakened by swans pecking on our cheeks, asking for their breakfasts. This was not like waking up in Greenwich Village. This was obviously the Promised Land that jazz players had always dreamed of.

This latter half of 1966 was the longest tour I've ever made in Europe. We were a hit. We made five European recordings within five months: *Ramblin'* (RCA Italiano), *Trio* (GTA), *Blood* (Fontana), *Prague Festival* (Supraphon), and *Haarlem* (Polydor).

At last I was in control of my own music. I did all the playing. No horns. I could finally put into practice *my* ideas of free jazz.

Why did Latin American music stop in the 1950s and not incorporate any of the innovations of jazz? Why did the classical music of India atrophy a thousand years earlier? Why did Spanish music only use one chord progression? This trio could open the window and breathe new life into traditions that had ground to a halt.

Recording has implications. Recorded performances become like a composer's opus numbers. For the next two years, back in new York, I would go into a recording studio on a regular basis, make an album and put it on the shelf. When Manfred Eicher came from Munich and visited my studio in New York for the first time in 1967, after looking at a room full, wall to wall, of master tapes, he said, "Paul, you are a record company just waiting to happen."

Manfred Eicher was a rare individual. As a former bassist, he had a group with cellist Thomas Stoewsand. When he decided to begin a record company he offered to buy some of my previously recorded music, resulting in ECM 1010 *Ballads*, with Gary Peacock and Barry Altschul. With that album it was my desire to do a project in which each ballad would be twenty-plus minutes long and be unlike the other ballads on the LP. At that time I was working on being the slowest pianist in the world. Manfred was always very helpful. We were on the same wavelength. He knew all there was to know about the intentions of the musicians he recorded.

Thoughout 1968 I worked in North America and released the album *Mr. Joy* (Mercury), with Gary Peacock and Billy Elgart, which was recorded at the University of Washington in Seattle. At the time I tried to sell in the United States, the *Blood* record released in Europe in 1966. So I visited the Mercury/Fontana office in New York with the LP under my arm. There was a large pile of records on the A&R guy's desk.

I said, "What are those?"

He said, "These are records from our European affiliates that they want us to release, but we prefer to release only the records that we record in New York."

I felt, here I was ready to give him the album for no advance, and decided that instead of offering him this record as I had intended, I would remake the album with a different trio, keeping exactly the same tunes and charging him a brand new fee. Deep down I wanted to punish this guy for not putting out what I considered my definitive album to date.

When I walked into the office, I didn't think that I could ever play these tunes as well again. But as it turns out, the remake with Peacock and Elgart was an improvement.

Paul Bley and Gary Peacock, New York, April 1963.
Photo by Len Dobbin.

12

Synthesizers
Moog – Peacock

WHEN IMPROVISERS left their previously acoustic domain and took up electricity, the intention in many cases was to make a literal translation of the acoustic music to electric. The inclusion of this new wealth of timbres produced an unexpected richness. Jaco Pastorius, unlike Stanley Clarke, chose to ignore the difficulties of mastering the acoustic bass because he believed the sound of the electric bass to be as valid as that of the acoustic bass.

In my case, the change from piano to electric keyboards, including the first primitive synthesizers, was to lead to results that I could not have fully predicted. One has only to examine the evolution of the sound of the electric guitar to realize that as the sound of an instrument changes, so will all the music that is made, solo or ensemble, with that instrument.

In ensemble playing, the thrill of losing oneself in an electric universe where the players may not be able to tell who is doing what, presented opportunities for real group integration. Unfortunately, many of my peers chose to ride the wave of instant popularity and large audiences that this electric sound offered, completely ignoring the advances of free jazz.

In 1969, I did an interview for *Down Beat* magazine. At the end of the interview, the writer casually asked what I thought about the new keyboard synthesizers. At this time, the keyboard had just been added to the synthesizer, so it was now perceived as being in my domain.

I said, "What's a keyboard synthesizer?"

He told me. Now I was interviewing him.

My next question was, "How do I get my hands on one?"

Bob Moog had just opened a factory in Trumansburg, New York, in the Finger Lakes district. I found out that there were only a few production models of the Moog synthesizer in existence, and that to get into the game you needed about twelve thousand dollars. But I decided I had to get this instrument.

When I phoned Trumansburg, it sounded even more difficult. In fact, there was only one production model in the factory, and several pianists and their wives and children had emigrated to Trumansburg, just because Bob would let them play it at three o'clock on Thursdays.

I sat down and wrote a script about a luncheon date between Paul Bley and Robert Moog. Although I'd never met the man, at the beginning of this one-act play I said "Hello, Bob" and he said "Hello, Paul," and at the end I drove off with a Moog synthesizer.

I called him up and told him I would like to come to Trumansburg to see him. He'd heard of me, at least enough to say come on up.

I understood that the synthesizer was a miniaturization of an electronic music studio, where composers laboriously spliced together hundreds of pieces of recording tape to create an electronically conceived musical composition. I pointed out to Bob that in reducing this roomful of equipment down to the size of a coffee table and adding a keyboard, he had not made any allowances for real-time performance. And I put it to Bob that his company was doomed to failure unless he had the input of a performing musician.

Bob went for it, but said that since there was only one production model in existence, he would have to ship it to me later.

I said, "That's not necessary, Bob. I have my rented station wagon just outside the door and if you grab a corner of the synthesizer we can carry it outside right now."

When we got back to New York, there were certain problems to be solved, since there was no instruction manual. Problem number one: how do you turn it on? Number two: How do you get it to make a sound? Number three: How do you get an attack and decay? Number four: How do you filter the sound?

This instrument required patching phono plugs between two places to make a connection. There were a million choices. For example, I learned that there were three kinds of vibrato: pitch vibrato as in a violin tremolo; volume vibrato, as if turning the volume knob up and down quickly; and timbre vibrato, as in turning the filtering knob up and down quickly. Since my hands were fully occupied with the keyboard and the patching, I had the luxury of designing twelve foot pedals for controlling these parameters.

In fact, only the instrument knew what it could do. It just sat there, pregnant with information. It took me and Annette two years to get to the point where we could give a performance on it. Finally, we found sound one. That was a nightmare, because once we'd found sound one, we had to go back and start again to find sound two. We literally spent two years or so drawing charts of the face of the instrument and the patch cording that was required for each desired sound and treatment. I had pretty much decided early on that I wanted the keyboard synthesizer to do things that the piano couldn't do.

With the synthesizer band we made some records. Between

Barry Altschul (drums), Glen Moore (bass), and
Paul Bley (Moog Synthesizer, Fender Rhodes), 1969.
Photo by Alain Bettex.

Paul Bley performing on his 'portable' Moog Synthesizer at
Philharmonic Hall, New York City, December 26, 1969.

April 1969, and October 1971 I made several synthesizer records. Annette Peacock did voice synthesis on some, and was the leader on one.

We played at the Jazz Workshop in Boston for a week—Barry Altschul and myself and a bassist—with this monophonic instrument with no memory. For a week! It was very hot stuff. I made tapes of it, but there was some very raw synthesizer playing, which we decided was too far out to be issued. As our technology grew, I found myself with several keyboards at my disposal. Photographs from that period show me stacking them. At that time, there was no precedent for putting one keyboard on top of another, what we now call the keyboard sandwich. I had to think of that by myself. There was no difference between the electric music and any of the free jazz we played acoustically. We didn't bother using the instrument to change the music; we were just hoping to be able to do some things that you couldn't do on acoustic instruments.

Annette assembled an instrument from additional Moog synthesizer modules that she could trigger using her voice, choosing the sounds she liked. She was plugging voice microphones into jacks that were looking for oscillator signals. That took even more work and the whole system became even less stable, because the instrument had zero memory. But she got some wonderful things.

I fondly remember a concert at the Village Vanguard. I had the synthesizer on the stage, a trio waiting to perform, an audience waiting for us to begin, and I was on the floor looking up under the synthesizer with a pocket flashlight and a screwdriver and the house mike, asking the audience to please bear with us. Max Gordon told me three things: get out, stay out, and don't come back. I haven't played the Vanguard since.

After doing the first live performance ever done with audio synthesizer and voice treatment at Philharmonic Hall on December 26th 1969, Annette and I received an offer to take the show to

Europe. I should have learned my lesson while I was lying on the stage of the Vanguard, but I was so excited about this instrument that I accepted the offer and went on the road.

The tour was with a quartet. I decided to buy a Volkswagen bus to get to the airport, because if we left it at the airport, we'd have a way to get back. It broke down, so we abandoned it on the Long Island Thruway and somehow made our way to the airport. We caught a plane to Luxembourg where we bought *another* Volkswagen bus which also broke down, and we abandoned it on the German autobahn. We finally caught a plane to Milan, but when we'd filled out the insurance form in New York we'd declared the true value of the equipment, so the customs inspector wanted the equivalent of about fifty thousand dollars cash as a deposit. However—and this could only happen in Italy—after I autographed one of my LPs for him, he waved us through.

We arrived in Milan, exhausted and half-crazed for the first date, and explained all our trials to the promoter. He looked at us and said, "You know, as far as I'm concerned, you could have just come and played the piano."

Once I finished that tour, including a performance at the Montreux Jazz Festival, that was it for electric instruments.

Annette's live performances, however, had drawn the attention of David Bowie, who was interested in singing with synthesizers as well. So around this time his Main Man Management office set up a loft for her on West Broadway and she moved out with our daughter Solo. She was now living in a 6,000 square foot loft with wall-to-wall astroturf. Main Man was managing her and they arranged for her first solo album *I'm the One*, which came out on RCA in 1972. Her career took off. Goodbye.

While I was coming down off the electronic experience in 1972, I was in Amsterdam with an acoustic trio and Manfred Eicher phoned

Annette Peacock and Paul Bley, *Jazz Hot* magazine,
October 1971.

me to inquire whether or not I was interested in making a solo piano record for ECM. My response was I had never attempted to play solo and that I would need a few days to think it over.

Subsequently, during a rehearsal of the trio, I was illustrating how the written music should go, and instead of stopping, I thought, this would be a good time to try to play the piano part without the trio. To my amazement, it was easier to play solo than it was to play trio. I telephoned Manfred and agreed to attempt a solo recording. This turned out to be the album *Open to Love*, part of the ECM solo piano recording series, which includes pianists Chick Corea and Keith Jarrett.

Playing the Arp Synthesizer.

13

The Fire

IN JANUARY 1973, I gave a small party at my home, and the guy who was redesigning my apartment brought as his date an artist named Carol Goss. It was love at first sight. I had just received the reel-to-reel tape from the solo piano session for ECM and I played it for her that night. Carol's background was in painting and theatre, but she'd also studied piano and her father had played saxophone with Woody Herman. I invited Carol to meet me in Europe that summer, and though she was working on the Billy Friedkin film, *The Exorcist*, she agreed to join me.

We met in Copenhagen, in front of the Club Montmartre, where I was playing with Niels-Henning Ørsted Pedersen. We recorded a duo album called NHOP that week also, which was my first album for Nils Winter's SteepleChase Records.

We spent a month touring Europe, at the end of which we stayed in ECM's traditional Japanese garden guest house in Munich. The morning Carol was due to fly back to New York, we had breakfast, left the dishes on the table, and went to the airport. When her flight was announced, I said, "Why don't I come with you to Frankfurt?—I'll see you off from there." At Frankfurt they shuffled us directly onto the New York flight without checking boarding passes, and I accompanied Carol back to New York, even though I was due to play a concert that weekend in Munich. Carol and I both realized that we had something very special to induce me to fly across an ocean because we didn't want to separate. To this day we haven't.

I had to purchase a full-price one-way ticket back to Munich and when I got back to the house, Manfred Eicher and Thomas Stoewsand, who worked for ECM at that time, said, "What happened? We came over, coffee was on the table, your clothes were in the closet, and there was no trace of you." Manfred told the story of my "disappearance" all over Europe for years.

After the European tour was over, I returned to New York. During the summer, Main Man had stopped paying Annette's loft rent and had dropped her from their roster. She was broke. She and Solo were being evicted and they were about to repossess her synthesizers. Solo was out in front of the loft building selling trinkets on the street. I thought this wasn't a good idea. I arranged for a truck to empty the apartment and put everything in storage and moved Annette and Solo back into the apartment on Hudson Street with me. Carol and I decided that we would have to take a break until Annette could sort her stuff out, which she did by moving to England with Solo a few months later.

Carol was from Miami and while visiting family there that winter she arranged for me to play synthesizer with a band at the planetarium where Jack Horkheimer of the PBS-TV astronomy show presides. That gig in Coconut Grove was fun. At one point during the show, just before the rocket was to be launched and we were to enter simulated outer space, someone would yell "Blast off!" at the top of their lungs and I would get the synthesizer to go to its lowest rumbling noise, which was a real window-rattler, and begin the slowest possible climb to the highest possible pitch that the human ear could hear. Its ability to do this was one of the things I liked about the synthesizer. Ross Traut, Danny Gottlieb, Danny

Rose, Tom Malone, and Bruce Ditmas joined me on that gig. We recorded at the planetarium, and WPBT-TV in Miami did a half-hour show of the band. It was while we were down in Miami that we met Jaco Pastorius for the first time.

Returning to New York, I was warned by my neighbor, who ran an auto paint shop next door, that while I'd been in Florida there had been three fires in the building in one week. Optimist that I was, I went upstairs and unpacked. For several days everything was quiet and it seemed that my optimism was justified.

Then one day around noon, I was asleep in the apartment when I heard a tremendous thundering crash as if an enormous old-growth tree had been uprooted and had fallen on the building. I was still half-asleep, but since there are no enormous old trees in Lower Manhattan, I knew instinctively that this sound meant trouble.

Smelling smoke, I made my way naked through the window and bars and onto the rear fire escape, which led directly on to the neighboring rooftop. Once on the roof, I felt safe, but then I remembered that I had forgotten my synthesizer. I turned around and went back for it. It was attached to its keyboard with heavy cabling, which I ripped apart. I dragged it to the rear window, this time through a heavy cloud of black smoke that made finding the window very difficult. I understand there's a kind of ecstasy that happens when you're overcome by smoke, in which you lose your perspective as to left and right and up and down. I finally found the window, but the synthesizer was a huge thing, and while I was getting it out onto the fire escape I managed to ram my right hand into the window frame, pushing the middle finger back about 180 degrees. When I finally got out onto the adjacent roof I noticed this and bent it back, hearing the bones click into place.

Once outside, I realized that I didn't have the synthesizer's keyboard. I went back in and went through the whole process again, not being able to tell where the rear window was, finally finding it, and getting out on the roof again.

Sitting there on the roof, my hand throbbing, I realized I was totally naked. This giant synthesizer was on my lap, and suddenly I felt very serene. Like leaving the hospital in Palm Springs, years before, I had just escaped death, and been rewarded with a moment of insight. The name of the game all along, I realized, was not acquiring possessions—after all, my home and everything in it was burning to the ground in front of me—but acquiring skills. In one sense I felt fulfilled, complete, very self-sufficient, but if I looked around at the world beyond me, I was clearly possessionless. In the end, I thought, you're only as wealthy as what is in your head. Material things can be taken away from you, but your skills and your judgment are yours forever.

I stayed on the roof until my friend who owned the paint shop came up, saw me naked, and got me a pair of overalls. The first thing I did when I got off the roof was go down to the garage and phone Carol. Her father had convinced me to take out an insurance policy on my equipment. I asked her if she had mailed it in yet. She said no, it was still sitting at the door. I asked her to please put it in the mail, immediately. So she did. I went over to her place, and we lived together from that evening on.

Ironically, I wasn't really interested in playing the synthesizer anymore and I had risked my life for it twice that day. It was totally charred and the keyboard melted. My shelves of tapes survived because they were in cardboard boxes. The boxes were all burnt on one side, but the tapes played fine. Carol got me to a specialist when my hand blew up like a balloon the next day. After X-rays it was decided that I was fine, just a little stiffness in the middle finger, which lasted for years.

14

Improvising Artists
Pastorius – Metheny

IMPROVISING ARTISTS INC. (IAI) was created in 1974 by myself and Carol Goss as an audio and video recording company in New York City. I was the audio producer and Carol was the art and video director. Improvising Artists: the name contains the philosophy.

I had just heard a tape of Dexter Gordon improvising on soprano in the dressing room of the Village Vanguard. When he wasn't onstage, he played very freely. In fact, I preferred it to his group playing. And I thought maybe we should dedicate a record company to the idea of very small ensembles—not necessarily with rhythm sections—and invite musicians who wanted to play free but had a lot of traditional background in composing and playing. So we invited people like Sun Ra and Sam Rivers and Lee Konitz to do just that. Our job was to start the tape rolling. We eventually put out twenty LPs.

Jimmy Giuffre, Bill Connors, Ran Blake, Mike Nock, Marion Brown, Perry Robinson, Oliver Lake, Lester Bowie, with Philip Wilson... Sam Rivers' records were duets with Dave Holland. I made an electric record with Jaco Pastorius and we picked up this promising young guitarist for the date—it turned out to be Pat Metheny's first recording. Of course, among those twenty records, each of those twelve to fifteen artists had a totally different approach to organizing a "free" ensemble record date.

That motivated the audio aspect of IAI. What motivated me in the video aspect was seeing a black-and-white videotape of Miles Davis playing in a theater in Philadelphia. It was the band with Cannonball Adderley, John Coltrane, Bill Evans, Paul Chambers, and Philly Joe Jones. It had been shot with a single camera on the first balcony, with a long lens so they could come in for closeups. The technique was to turn to the left for the piano solo, to the right for rhythm section solos, and to the center for the horn solos. It was absolutely astounding. I realized that, regardless of the fidelity of the sound, or of the picture, I was getting an incredible amount of information. As a player, if I'd been listening to a record of that band I might get twenty thousand bits of information, but with visuals I was now getting two million bits per second. I realized that video was a tremendous archival and educational resource.

Carol took the idea of video much further than I had anticipated. After Nam June Paik recommended that she check out the Experimental Television Center in Binghamton, New York, in 1974 she started making and exhibiting abstract video art programs. She also brought video synthesizers to gigs in New York and San Francisco and did live performance video with the bands throughout the 1970s.

The players loved the opportunity to make a record date—and doing it for another musician gave them a kind of security, because my technique as a producer was to bolt the door to keep out the producers.

I had learned this from Nat Hentoff when he worked for Candid Records in the fifties and sixties. He had produced the Don Ellis session that I had done with Steve Swallow in 1961. At that time, producers were known as A&R men, meaning that the personnel of the band and the compositions that they played were entirely under their control. They were authority figures who came to the session with a whole agenda for you, regardless of what your interests were at that time. They were the employer. In general, producers were not musicians, they just had an idea of what might sell records. Hentoff's approach to A&R was to barricade the door to the studio so that no one could come and disturb us. Then he sat down and read the entire Sunday *New York Times* from cover to cover. He was the perfect producer, because he knew not to offer the musicians any help unless they asked for it, and they almost never did.

There is a whole psychology about recording improvisation. The best way to make an album is leave the musicians alone and to record every note from the sound check to the end of the session and then release the album with the tunes in the order they were played.

Carol and I started IAI out of our apartment on Jane Street. It was a studio, and we had three employees and a telex machine in the closet that went off with a huge racket at four in the morning while we were sleeping. We enlisted the help of a longtime friend of Carol's, David Good, who managed the sales and shipments of the records. We found that in the record business, 24 hours a day is not enough time. You need at least 44! It took two hours to open the day's mail. Not to read it, just to open it and flatten the pages in sequence. It was an incredible amount of work, but we had a lot of fun.

The first recording we made was *Quiet Song* with Jimmy Giuffre, guitarist Bill Connors, and myself. It won the Prix de Jazz in France in 1976. The sixth record was all electric and included Jaco Pastorius, bass; Pat Metheny, guitar; Bruce Ditmas, drums; and myself on Fender Rhodes electric piano.

When we met Jaco in Miami in April 1974, he was the local bass guitar star. Although he was unknown outside of Florida, his playing impressed me enough for us to invite him to come to New York to do a gig and record that June. When he arrived in New York City, he had brought with him a large speaker-amp and when I asked him why he went to all that trouble on the flight, when he could have more easily rented one in New York, he said, "This is my *sound*, man."

At rehearsals I noticed that he never stopped playing and fingering the electric bass, even when the amp was off. He had so much energy that he would run across the street and play basketball when the band took a break.

The opening night of the quartet's debut in a week-long engagement at the Cafe Wha in the Village was full of surprises. After the first set, we took an intermission and I went into the audience to sit with friends, who after a while commented, shouldn't I be on the bandstand playing, since the other three members of the band were still onstage? I protested that since I was the leader and it was an intermission, if they wanted to remain on the stage that was their prerogative, but I was going to take my break.

It turned out that they were so excited playing this first-time recreation of the free jazz period on electric instruments that they didn't want to miss a minute of it. Up until this point no one had made the translation of the free period to electric. The sonic possibilities of electricity fit perfectly with the purposes of free jazz. Coupled with the rhythmic virtuoso drive of Pastorius and Ditmas, this band was hot. After the first tune, guitarist Ross Traut asked me if a friend of his, a student of the Berklee School of Music, could sit in on guitar.

I said, "Ross, it's your gig, if you want someone to sit in it's okay with me." Pat Metheny sat in and sat in and sat in for the rest of the week. The later recording of this band recorded at Blue Rock Studio on June 16, 1974, and released by IAI was both Jaco and Pat's first recorded studio date.

Bley and Ran Blake on Improvising Artists
tour of Europe.
Photo by Roberto Massotti.

Paul Bley and Carol Goss co-producing *Quiet Song*, the
first recording for Improvising Artists, November 14, 1974.

The idea of translating the free acoustic repertoire to electric was an idea the public was waiting to hear. Having a label that we owned could have easily allowed me to make another ten records of this format with these and other electric players. I chose not to do this, because I had come to a crossroads in my life. I was faced with the decision of whether to spend the rest of my days being an acoustic pianist or an electric one. And since everyone at that time, including Joe Zawinul, Herby Hancock, and Chick Corea were all playing electric music, I thought there would be no one left to play acoustic piano. Besides, I already knew how to play electric.

Improvising Artists produced a number of concerts and tours at various times for the artists that we were recording. Sun Ra was performing with the large Arkestra in the seventies, but we decided that it was time to record him solo piano. So IAI booked a European two-piano tour for Sonny and me. While we were traveling by train in Italy, just outside of Bologna, it started to snow. Since the conductor was not familiar with snow, he stopped the train outside of town. We only had an hour to the next concert in Florence. Sonny said he was "waiting for a sign" as to how to solve our predicament. I'd asked others on the train how much a cab was to Florence and they said a hundred dollars, so I went up to Sonny and I said, "Sonny, we've just received a sign, the taxi's waiting."

Sonny and I would each do a separate solo set at each concert. When the concert was over and we were called for an encore, we did a four-handed piano piece. Sonny played the treble end, which left me the bass.

We did the record date with Sonny at a club called Axis in Soho on West Broadway on May 20, 1977. David Baker, who audio engineered most of the IAI sessions, brought in equipment to record the sound. Carol brought in a video crew from the Kitchen and the Experimental Television Center to shoot video.

One of the issues that Carol had been addressing with her

abstract video work was how to make a video that would bear the same repeatability as a music record. The nature of analog video synthesizers meant that these abstract images were made continuously, in real time and then coupled with music afterwards. Initially, her primary criterion for the union of video and audio was the length of the track. The amazing thing was that these supposedly random joinings worked and seemed inevitable. They would have many points of synchronization, both rhythmically and thematically. Carol found that abstract images in motion had many direct corollaries with free jazz. Though some of the Dadaist and Cubist painters had made abstract animated films earlier in the century, it was only after 1968 and the advent of videotape that artists could make painterly images move in real time, much as musicians make sound move through time.

Interestingly, at the same time that Jaco was playing feedback on the speaker amp of his electric bass, Carol and other video artists of the period were experimenting with analog video feedback. She also made several tapes where audio oscillators are visualized on the screen. One such program was "Topography," which contained an electric quartet of mine with Bill Connors on electric guitar, which has never been released on CD. That program premiered at the Everson Museum of Art's "New Work in Abstract Video" show in Syracuse, New York in 1976, and then toured the U.S., Europe, and Japan.

The nature of exhibition and private viewing was different than that of live performance. There was no precedent for the production of abstract and synthesized images in real time during performance when Carol brought video in that weekend at Axis in Soho.

We made three video performance recordings that weekend. The first two with Sun Ra, one solo, and the other with John Gilmore, Ahmed Abdullah, Danny Davis, Eddie Thomas, and June

Tyson. The third was made with me and Glen Moore, the acoustic bass player with Oregon.

Carol made these programs in collaboration with video artist Walter Wright. They included completely free camera movement, feedback, and colorization on David Jones' analog video synthesizer. Sun Ra was a willing collaborator—his theatrical sensibility suited the stretching of realism, which the video synthesizers were capable of. But more important than that is the fact that the images were being improvised simultaneously with the music. The entire vocabulary of improvisation was being adopted by the video artists. Instead of using the traditional top-down hierarchy of the broadcasting world, the video artists played independently, with the screen as their "speaker," where their group sensibilities were being mixed and displayed.

At the *Reeds 'n Vibes* session with Marion Brown and Gunter Hampel, Carol recorded the session through the Dan Sandeen analog video synthesizer, alternating tracks between natural, realistic images and images that were keyed and abstracted with synthesized colors.

The last audio recording for IAI was made at a performance at the Great American Music Hall in San Francisco in 1978, with Jimmy Giuffre, Lee Konitz, Bill Connors, and myself.

At that performance, the video crew arrived with ten times the cable of the audio crew. There was a large projection screen on the stage for the audience. Initially, the camera people—Carol, who was directing and taking turns at the switcher and Bill Hearn's analog Video Lab synthesizer, and Skip Sweeney—all wore head-phones and mikes so that they could communicate with one another during the shoot. In the first piece, she decided to discard the phones because the delay between her call and the camera person's getting the shot made the camera work late. The music was all improvised, and so if a camera person waited for a cue before going for a shot they would miss a solo. When everyone was liberated from cues, no one was "late," everyone was participating equally in the moment.

In fact, the whole concept of editing, so integral to traditional television and film production, was discarded. There was a distinct loss of integrity when a live video performance was dismembered and then reassembled. Carol decided that the video artists would play for keeps, just as the musicians did.

The real decisions being made were ones about aesthetics. How much realism, how much abstraction? When does the color palette change? Should the video play in counterpoint to the music or be supportive? Most of the video work done in the 1970s and 1980s was documentary in nature, so that the few artists who approached video as a painterly art form were pretty much on a first-name basis. Also, there were no strict genres established in the 1970s.

Carol produced abstract and performance video recordings for six of the twenty records and numerous short video pieces with single tracks from the other albums as audio accompaniment. Stills from her videos were used on many of the IAI LP covers. Improvising Artists was credited, on the cover of *Billboard* magazine in 1978, with creating the first "music videos."

As a musician, it turned out that running a record company created a bit of a dilemma with other labels. Had I approached them for a record date, they would have said, "Hey, record for your own label! Why are you calling me?" So, for seven years, I became exclusively an IAI artist. One thing I did get from IAI is that now when I talk to a record company, I understand the nature of the transaction from both sides. I've learned that people who run jazz record companies are patrons of the art and by and large should be regarded as saints!

I've always tried to do things just to do them so I could put them behind me, and over those seven years, Carol and I found

Yamaha Music Festival, Nemu No Sato, Japan 1976
Paul Bley (piano), Gary Peacock (bass), and
Barry Altschul (drums) on Improvising Artists tour.
Photo by Carol Goss.

that, yes indeed, we could run a record company. Once we knew that, running a record company became a little less interesting. Also, both of us wanted to concentrate more on our own work.

Solo piano concert, L'Opéra de Lyon,
Lyon, France, October 5, 1996.
Photo by Renaud Vezin.

15

Reunions
Guild – Baker – Giuffre

I HAD A FANTASY about living in a Brazilian rain forest—but in a house with a satellite dish, computers, and fax machine. Inside, you're the hub of a worldwide communication network, but as soon as you step outside you've got alligators, swamps, and huge exotic birds. Extreme contrast is very important.

Failing that, Carol and I, after running Improvising Artists throughout the seventies, got married and moved to upstate New York in the eighties. Angelica, our first daughter, was born in Cherry Valley in 1980. We spent many winters in Miami, where Vanessa, our second daughter, was born in 1985.

Miami had always been a draw for me ever since I hitchhiked down in the winter as a teenager from Montreal, stopping at "all you can drink" orange juice stands along the way. I made many friends down there, such as reed player Keshavan Maslak, with whom I've recorded. Some, like Hammond B3 player Jeff Palmer, drummer Richard Poole, and hand drum player, Darwin Davis, I've had a hand in transplanting to the northeast.

It seemed appropriate that our permanent home in the mountains of New York was something of a center for American poetry, because I've known a lot of poets. I've always been able to relate to the fact that a poet is somebody who has to choose the disastrous course for his life, because he can make poems out of it. You can't give a poet good advice—that would be counter-productive to his output. If a poet said to you that he was going to become a merchant seaman, there's no reason to start giving him fatherly advice, because without even knowing it, he's generating stories for the future.

Allen Ginsberg's Committee on Poetry owned a building high in the mountains outside of the village, and for years he maintained an open house for poets to come and stay, which is how poet Charlie Plymell found this house and wound up selling it to me. All the American poets have been here at one time or another during the summer months. Isolation is no problem—there is no phone.

After we stopped being active with IAI, my performance career really went into high gear, partly because of what running a record company had taught me about the needs and wants of the music industry. In fact, soon my daughters were growing up without having me around for six months of the year. Thirty concerts a year used to be a good year. Now I have to work just as hard to give myself thirty days off.

I had such good luck with reunions on Improvising Artists that I welcomed the idea of recording once again with many of the musicians I'd played with earlier on. One of the first of these reunions was actually a film.

Imagine the Sound was made for theatrical exhibition in 1981. It had four different segments: Bill Dixon and his group, Archie Shepp and his. Cecil Taylor played solo and I played solo. Ron Mann co-produced this film with Bill Smith, who was the editor of *Coda Magazine* and co-owner of Sackville Records. Mann directed and Smith interviewed us. They flew us in for a week each, consecutively, to make our segments. The film contained some music, some poetry and a lot of interviews. The four of us had been an integral part of the Jazz Composer's Guild of the 1960s.

When I got to see the the premiere at the Bleecker Street Theater in New York, it turned out that, in spite of lengthy interviews with each of the musicians, no one ever mentioned that there even *was* a Jazz Composer's Guild. In fact, the liner notes to the *Imagine the Sound* laser disc don't mention the Guild either, just that we were "four musicians influential in the evolution of free form jazz in the late '50s and early '60s."

In the early 80s, the promoter of the Antibes Jazz Festival liked to put together artists he thought might play well together and he recommended that Chet Baker and I play a duo at Antibes. We hadn't played together since the '50s. When I got there, they told me the sound check was going to be at four o'clock. I knew immediately that Chet was not going to make any sound check—he never made any sound checks. So I went to his hotel and instead of rehearsing or having a soundcheck I had a long talk with him and his girlfriend.

Antibes is an outdoor festival and quite large. Chet and I played ballads for the whole hour and the audience was absolutely quiet and very attentive; they loved it. I was amazed that you could do an outdoor music festival and play really quiet if you had the hypnotic capacity in the music you made.

After that Nils Winter suggested that Chet and I make a record together, which was called *Diane*, after Chet's tune. We recorded it on February 2, 1985. There was some trepidation about Chet, but he showed up exactly on time and very together. We tried a tune and he stopped me in the middle and said, "You know Paul, listen. I can only play things that I can *sing*." It seems that I was playing with a little too much technique.

And he said, "I can only play jazz solos that I can sing."

I said, "Chet. You only have a six-note range." Which was supposedly a joke, but in fact, I had to play very minimally for Chet. Even more minimally than my minimalism, which turned out to be a very good discipline.

Some time after that I was invited to play at the Festival International de Jazz de Montréal in a duet with Chet Baker. I learned that they carefully monitored Chet's travel plans from Liège, Belgium, so that they knew exactly when he was on the train to Paris, when he caught the flight to Canada, when he arrived at the airport in Montreal, and so on. He was then picked up and brought to his hotel at the festival. I met him in the hotel and we went looking for some refreshments. Then we went looking for more refreshments. When it came time for the concert, it was sold out and the press was in attendance.

When I spoke with Chet just before the concert, I said that he seemed a little under the weather.

I said, "Why don't I go out and play some solo, and I'll call you and you can come out?"

So I played two tunes. I was surprised when Chet walked out on the stage in the middle of the second tune. He sat down on a high stool overlooking the orchestra pit, looking out into the audience. I thought, well, maybe he wants to play. So I finished the tune and went over to him and said, "Chet, how are ya doin'? What do you wanna play?" He mentioned the name of a tune... I went back to the piano and played an introduction and he didn't come in. I played the introduction again. He didn't come in. So I went over to him and said, "Chet, maybe you don't like this tune. Why don't we play another tune?"

We discussed it and I went over and played an introduction again. But this time the audience was yelling, "Get off the stage!" and "Go home, Chet!" and so forth.

So since he didn't come in after a couple more introductions I went up to him and said, "Well, Chet, let's take a break. We'll take an intermission," realizing that he was in no shape to do the gig.

When we got off the stage, I told them to call up the promoter on the cell phone. He came right over. He locked Chet in his dressing room till the end of the set. I had to go back out on the stage and face the audience. I finished the concert solo. That was the last time I saw Chet.

In 1989 the editor of *Jazz Magazine* in Paris, Phillipe Carles, contacted Jean-Jacques Pussiau, owner of Owl Records, and suggested it might be time for a reunion of the Jimmy Giuffre Trio. It had been thirty years since our recordings for Verve and CBS. Time flies when you're having fun. As we expected, the sparks were all there. Steve Swallow was now playing electric bass guitar. Jimmy had been able to adapt his unique subtone sound to additional instruments: flutes, soprano sax, as well as clarinet and tenor. I had so much of Giuffre's contrapuntal group in my head during the last thirty years that when the other two guys stopped playing I could play both their parts simultaneously. The fur was flying. Giuffre was received all over Europe at the highest level and we enjoyed the rewards that we had waited so long for.

Juanita Giuffre, who was a composer in her own right, would accompany us everywhere on tour. I remember one afternoon at a sound check in the Roman amphitheater in Verona, Italy—stone seats and all. Giuffre handed out some of his music. Just then, a violent Shakespearean storm broke. The winds took the written music and scattered them to the air. Juanita turned to Giuffre and said, "I guess this must be a sign that this is the end of written music." I've never played a note of written music since.

My fondest memory of this group is traveling to a chateau in southern France by plane, where we were being filmed for a feature on Giuffre. At the airport we requested three wheelchairs, and to this day, I regret that we did not take advantage of this photo op.

The Jimmy Giuffre Trio, Verona, Italy, 1992.
Steve Swallow, Jimmy Giuffre, Paul Bley.
Photo by Elena Carminati.

16

The Road

WHEN I BEGAN TOURING a lot, I decided to just carry a shoulder bag—no charts, no instruments, no rehearsals, no sound checks, no program. When it comes to recording, not having an agenda means that we can do the music in real time, in the order in which it's going to be released. All of this is based on an on-the-road lifestyle. You just don't have any time, so you learn to do everything on the first take. You don't have a year to listen, mix, and assemble. It's anti-electronic, because electronic music always demands months of overdubs. And in a sense it's very traditional—the tradition of the jazz touring band.

When I go to a studio and they ask for a sound check, I tell them that the sound check is going to be the first tune of the album. In fact, they have to have a sound check before we make the sound check. So now, there are no more sound checks. Sound checks and rehearsals are wasted notes, wasted intensity.

It was a period of simplification. Not touching an instrument between concert tours and recordings resulted in my developing a strong appetite for adding opus numbers to my recorded repertoire.

Making music for other labels was much easier than running a record company. Recording an entire CD as a single concept was a way of documenting my progress in developing a language for playing solo piano.

In 1982, I was on my way to Europe and I thought to bring a master tape to Giovanni Bonandrini, owner of Soul Note Records in Milan. We had an appointment. Giovanni was dapper, dressed in his Italian pinstriped double-breasted suit. Giovanni is a former school teacher and a record collector who wound up acquiring the Soulnote/Black Saint Label from a fellow who had gone bankrupt. I arrived at the studio with Jeff Palmer, the Hammond B3 organist I was bringing to Europe for the first time. I handed Giovanni the tape and he loaded it on to the machine and there was nothing but hiss, just tape noise. I was surprised and we waited and waited.

Giovanni said, "Well, maybe it's further into the tape." So he fast forwarded, and the same situation: hiss, hiss, hiss. Then he said, "We'll reverse the tape" The same thing happened again.

As soon as Giovanni realized what had happened he fell to the floor in paroxysms of laughter. I was somewhat shocked that he was thrashing his legs on the floor and laughing and I was worried about him. When he finally recovered and saw the perplexed look on my face he said, "Don't worry Paul, we'll do the album any-way." In all his years of being in the record business, no one had ever crossed the ocean to bring him a *blank* tape.

I did a tour of Latin America in 1983. When I arrived at the airport in Rio, I was picked up by a taxi driver who took me to the top of Pao de Acucar, the mountain with the huge statue of Christ. As the sun came up he pulled out his trumpet and played. Everyone made music in Rio. The next night I was taken to a tango palace. The men and women lined up on opposite sides of the room. No one was smiling. This was serious. When the tango music started, they would walk out and meet their partners in the middle of the dance floor. When the music stopped, they went back to their opposite sides. I learned that if you leave roses on someone's doorstep, to the right it means one thing, to the left it means another.

From Rio, I flew to Miami to join Carol and Angelica for a few days before continuing on to Europe. Rio had infused me with so much joy that I picked up Angelica, who was two years old at the time, and danced with her for hours. When I played in Milan a few weeks later, I recorded the solo piano album, *Tango Palace* for Soul Note Records.

Occasionally, I've had the family on the road, and though I was not initially enthralled with the idea, it has provided some memorable experiences. We returned from a vacation in Miami one winter to discover that pipes were frozen right out to the street. The water couldn't be turned on. The only solution was for Carol and Angelica to come to Europe with me. We found a great apartment in Paris on rue de Sevigné and stayed for three months. We occasionally frequented a restaurant in the Marais, where Angelica, age three, would dance in the aisles to the accompaniment of the house guitarist and banjo player, playing in the style of Django Reinhardt. In fact, it was at the 100th birthday celebration of Django, that the jazz critic, Maurice Cullaz, who was in his seventies at the time, proposed to Angelica, saying that he could never resist a dancer.

A decade later, to get to the Halifax Jazz Festival in 1994, Carol and I drove to Boston with Angelica and Vanessa and then took a flight up to Nova Scotia. There were two Steinways on the stage. Jon Ballantyne played a set on one piano, and then I did a set on the other piano. We played several encores in duet with the two pianos. The whole concert was broadcast by the CBC. After the gig was over and the house filed out, Vanessa, who was nine at the time, went up to Jon's piano and improvised for twenty minutes without a break. I think, because of his youth, she felt that it was acceptable to sit in his chair and "continue" the concert.

IAI brought a group of musicians over for a European tour in 1978. In Italy, we hired a sound truck to record one of the concerts, and two things happened. One was that Lee Konitz wondered whether I noticed a card table set up back of the sound truck, with a guy sitting there with these headphones and a tape recorder? We went over and looked to see what it was and, sure enough, there was some pirate, taping the gig that I was paying a sound truck for. When we got back to the U.S. with that tape we found out that there were cricket sounds all over it and they were as loud as the band.

Strangely enough, the same thing happened in Martinique while I was touring with John Surman, Paul Motian, and Bill Frisell. Carol had flown in from New York to meet me there midway through the tour. She shot some video of the band on the way to the gig and during the gig as well. It was 98.6 degrees Fahrenheit outside, and humid. The concert was in a theater that didn't have air conditioning. All the doors to the hall had to be left open. Just as we started to play at sunset the crickets and frogs started to tune up outside, thousands of them. They're all over the tape, of course.

Thomas Stoewsand, who booked that tour, tried to put a really great gig in the middle of a long tour. We flew out from Paris to Martinique in February. It was so great, that after the Martinique concert, Surman told Thomas, "If you get any more work, just call my answering machine and leave the date and the location and the fee. But if you get another gig in Martinique, just leave the date."

To be a road warrior, you need an unclubable sense of humor. No matter what the difficulties are—and there are unforeseen difficulties nightly—you have to have an attitude that it's all going to work out. Some of the best people that I've worked with on the road have survived unforeseen events by being able to be funny about it. So there we were, Paul Motian and I, in Macedonia at seven o'clock on a Sunday morning, waiting for our Macedonian van driver to drive us to the airport to get a flight to Paris, where we had a concert that night. An hour went by and there was no trace of the driver. Everyone was asleep at the hotel, nobody was stirring, and we realized that this guy was not coming. We had to wake some of the hotel personnel to finally get a ride, but Paul and I realized that the only way to guarantee a van driver showing up that early in the morning was to not just get *his* phone number, but to get the phone number of his girlfriend as well.

The road is always unpredictable. In 1976, IAI took my trio with Gary Peacock and Barry Altschul to Japan. We toured the islands for the entire month of August. One gig was at the Yamaha Music Foundation's resort for its employees in Nemu-no-Sato on the southeast coast. It was so hot and humid that our eyeglasses were fogged over. Carol and I went down to the executives' club to have dinner before the gig, which wasn't until midnight. We ordered lobster. When the food arrived, it was beautifully arranged on a wooden board. They placed it in front of us. Just as we were about to try some, the antennae of the lobster started to move. We looked at each other and called the waiter. He explained that this way the guests knew the lobster was fresh.

We hit at midnight for 10,000 people in an outdoor amphitheater. Our gig that night was broadcast and later released on IAI as *Japan Suite*.

Even back in 1961, during my first trip to Europe with the Jimmy Giuffre Three, we had met a lot of European jazz musicians, who at the time were playing bebop. It was only in 1965 that free music had caught on like wildfire in Europe and there were many German, Scandinavian, and French groups playing free. There were also a lot of jazz schools in Europe, so the amount of musicians and the level of the musicians kept going up and up. Now, if you are looking at each of the instruments, there are several European contenders on all the instruments who would rank with the best American musicians.

I've made records with a number of these musicians, primarily for European labels. Steve Lake, a journalist who was working at ECM, suggested in 1994 that we might want to make a date with a trio I was getting ready to tour with, which included Evan Parker, tenor and soprano saxophone, and Barre Phillips, bass. I had heard a lot about Evan Parker's exceptional ability to play with circular breathing. That was a facility that had been around for a long time. Even back in the thirties, members of the Duke Ellington Orchestra could circular breathe for a short time, and Giuffre could as well. But Evan was famous for being able to circular breathe almost indefinitely. He could even speak while circular breathing, which he did with me on several occasions. So we started a piece on the record date when we first met and he went into circular breathing and I was disconcerted about somebody who could play all the time without even taking a breath, until I realized that I could circular breathe with both hands at the piano.

André Menard, the artistic director of the Festival International de Jazz de Montréal, invited me to play there in 1989. That trio concert with Charlie Haden and Paul Motian was released by Verve Records. After that, the festival did a "Paul Bley Homage" with four nights of concerts in July of 1992. This included a solo concert, a duo concert with John Scofield, a trio performance with Gary Peacock and Billy Hart, and a trio performance with John Surman and Paul Bollenbeck. I invited saxophonist Joe Maneri to come down to the festival and do a final closing set. His son, Matt Maneri, played electric violin and I joined them on piano and Kurzweil. In 1995, I performed solo piano at the festival. Some of those concerts were

Paul, Carol, Angelica, and Vanessa, 1990.

Charlie Haden, Paul Motian, Paul Bley.
Photo by Hans Harzhelm.

videotaped.

Jim West of Justin Time Records in Montreal often recorded me when I came to Montreal for the Jazz Festival. There was a reunion date with Herbie Spanier in 1993, on which Geordie McDonald played percussion. These dates with Canadian musicians included several first-time duet encounters with Kenny Wheeler, trumpet; with Sonny Greenwhich, guitar; and Jane Bunnett, soprano sax and flute.

In 1998, while making a biographical film for ARTE-TV for Europe, I invited Jane Bunnett to play soprano saxophone with me in duet on several of the pieces. We hung out that night and closed a couple of bars together and she told me about the difficulty she was having getting Cuban musicians into the United States for an upcoming tour. When they first came to Toronto to rehearse, they would stay up all night rehearsing at her place and then she and her husband would send them to their hotel rooms in a taxi. An hour later, they would be right back in her apartment. It seems that they were so communal that they didn't want to be alone.

Usually the opposite is true. When on the road for a month with 28 flights, time alone is a luxury. The road is work. The gig is play. A recent fax sent home from the Montreux Festival en route to Istanbul and Spain, read:

> Last night Charlie Haden's bass arrived in two pieces, with the neck detached from the body. Lee Konitz's keys on the alto saxophone were stuck and he needed some rubber bands in the middle of a televised sax solo.... Fires breaking out in 100 degrees plus temperatures all over southern Europe. As usual, touring is a 'pressure.'

17

Update

IN AUGUST 1993, I was invited by Ralph Simon of Postcard Records to make a solo synthesizer record. The instrument was digital; there was memory, a large selection of presets, and compared to the analog days, it was a breeze. The day before the session, I invited the owner of the Kurzweil synthesizer I played on the session, Dan Stein, to join me at my hotel to select the sounds I would be needing. The following day, we went into the recording studio—twenty-two years after my last synthesizer recording in 1971. I went to the date fully thinking that all of my choices of sounds would work equally well, only to find to my dismay that after recording for six hours and returning to the hotel for playbacks, I only liked one four-minute track.

The question was, what was there about this one tape that was different from the five hours of unsuccessful music I had recorded that day? It turned out that what worked best was triggering a very long electronic sequence on the synthesizer by pressing just a few notes and then chasing the electronic music with the acoustic piano. And so for the remainder of the date, we followed this procedure. The album, with one day's preparation, earned the first *Down Beat* five-star review for Postcard Records and I've often wondered since then what would have happened if I had had the synthesizer for two days before the record date.

During this period, I was walking down Seventh Avenue in Greenwich Village, when I met saxophonist Hayes Greenfield, who asked me if I'd ever been to a club called The Cooler in the meat market section on West 14th Street near the Hudson River. I was hesitant about going to an area frequented by hookers who plied their trade amongst truckers and were known for being able to keep a razor blade under their tongue while performing fellatio.

The sign in front of the club merely said, "Live Jazz Tonight." No mention of artists. A van pulled up and the musicians unloaded their instruments, including a large video projection screen. When the band began to play in a darkened room, they played for one hour—very free, very electric, very continuous, accompanying a pretty primitive series of travelog-like video images. It occurred to me that I was witnessing what could easily be a CD video. What was curious about this performance was not that the musicians were performing with video, but that they were performing without video artists.

Electricity is taken for granted, but its implications for musicians keep changing. Video is one of those implications. In 1996, Carol Goss organized the Not Still Art Festival, "to create a forum for video artists working in abstract and non-narrative electronic motion imaging in conjunction with musicians and sound artists." By 1998 nearly one third of the video programs in the national screening were made by artists who described themselves primarily as musicians. As she wrote in the program:

> The experience that musicians had in the '70s when they couldn't distinguish who was playing what because the electric environment allowed them all to simulate each others sound, now exists equally for video artists and musicians. They were using the same analog elements and

electronic production concepts in the 1970s, but the tools were still differentiated.

In the 1980s, as all electronic art migrated from analog to digital instruments, visual artists and musicians found themselves both sitting at computers and sharing the same software environment. There was no longer any necessary division between these realms of creativity.

In the fall of 1998 I received a fax from the American Physical Society. They were putting together a Centennial Time Line for 1999, celebrating 100 years of accomplishments in physics. They asked for a photo of me playing the Moog synthesizer at Philharmonic Hall in New York City, 1969. They claim that I was the first to adapt the analog keyboard synthesizer for live performance.

The responsibility for the future of electronic art now rests with the instrument makers, and the programmers, who must serve artists/musicians by making software that allows for interactivity *and* performance, which is at the heart of improvisation and jazz.

The future of jazz will depend on how well it plays with visuals, and to a great extent, that will be the responsibility of the players. The video that we recorded from 1974 to the present will finally be released on video disc formats that provide audio quality equal to, or better than CDs. The Improvising Artists website— www.improvart.com—will distribute long-format audio and video. Musicians have a lot more on their plates than ever before.

In 1993, through the invitation of my old friend Ran Blake, I was invited to teach at the New England Conservatory in Boston, where Jimmy Giuffre had been teaching for years. Jazz has only been taught in academia since the 1960s, so it's still very much a new frontier.

I don't consider myself to be teaching jazz. Mostly, I try not to teach what people already like to do. The part of the music that they don't want to talk about is what I try to teach. Students show up at the Conservatory wanting to become jazz musicians and asking if there is a placement bureau for when they graduate. I tell them the phone isn't going to ring—what are you going to do then?

I had been very much against teaching. The problem I had was that from the teachers I had met, it seemed there was more to be lost by being a student than to be gained. If a student has a charismatic teacher, a dependency situation can develop, similar to the one that occurred when John Mehegan was running a jazz class at Juilliard and invited me to play as a guest. I noticed that the students were in love with him and in some cases were paying for the social relationship rather than the music lessons.

I only agreed to do two days per month, long enough to get a good lobster at Legal Seafood. The students were professional musicians in their twenties and thirties, from the United States, Europe, Israel, and Asia. I was teaching one-on-one with them, not in classes. Each one had a totally different set of needs and a totally different story. They could already play. All my students were very professional, but they all had personal needs that were not being addressed. So sometimes I dealt with immigration, sometimes I dealt with financing through their families, sometimes I dealt with love affairs. What they all needed was an ego boost.

In the case of a Japanese student, Satoko Fuji, who was told she could not play unless she could play like Bud Powell, I offered her two choices: we could either spend two years learning to play like Bud Powell or we could start making free records. She chose the latter. Now she has CDs out on four record labels. Going into the recording studio was the best thing I could do with my students. Sometimes we would record at the school and sometimes outside the school. Rather than spend a lot of time telling them the details of music, we could move along a lot faster if we just made a record. I could also help them begin a self analysis, a self-correcting situation, so that after they left school they could continue to record on a regular basis, every couple of months. In this way, they could be their own teacher and they wouldn't develop any dependencies.

One way or another, the demands of being a performing musician are greater now than they ever were. You need to develop your musical talent to the utmost, and having the business smarts of the CEO of a major corporation won't hurt at all. So mostly, I try to tell the students how to get a job—although I myself haven't asked for work since 1964.

The 1990s have been a brand new ball game for all artists. Musically, the seventies and the eighties were dead decades compared to the fifties and sixties. Everyone feels that something is coming, and what's coming next is what has always interested me. The one thing you can be sure of is that you won't like it.

In my career, the maximum length of an audio recording has gone from three minutes to 72 minutes—and on video, a performance can be documented for several hours.

What I suggested to the students at NEC is what I had learned in the early sixties. At the Mercury Wing record date, Bob Shad said I was pacing the floors between tunes, since it was only my second record date and I was nervous. I realized: why did I have to go into a professional recording studio with a professional label to record? I could hire the recording studio myself and stockpile tapes. If I needed an album, I could just go to the shelf and pull the "best of" off the shelf. That would solve the problem of nervousness. So I started a lifelong process of recording, whether it was for someone else or not. And as it is now I have hundreds of hours of professional recording sessions, most of which have never been released.

In a year, I make one recording for SteepleChase, one for Soul Note, one for ECM, one for Justin Time, one for BMG, and so on, and I would not give up these relationships for anything in the world.

But that is why I'm so prolific. Improvising is really a snapshot of who you are the month that you make the record. In that snapshot, as in all snapshots, you never look the same as you did last year.

When I go onstage to play solo, I don't get stuck. I can play for an hour, an hour and a half, with a repertoire or without a repertoire. I have so much to draw upon now that I really don't worry about it. And I'm constantly interested in taking different ethnic musics and adding them to what I do. Especially if I'm coming to the stage without anything. In Madrid or Tokyo, the local music becomes very influential and I find it often comes out in the performance and then goes toward building future repertoire.

Solo piano is different from playing in a group and it's also different from solo playing on other instruments. Each historical period has been identified by an almost totally different way of playing the piano. Stride and cakewalk used the left hand playing swing bass. The left hand was actually more active than the right.

Almost all the way through bebop, the piano was an imitator of saxophones and trumpets. The left hand lost its function for the most part and became just a snare drum, putting accents into the right-hand saxophone part. Then Bill Evans and George Shearing thickened that saxophone/trumpet part on the piano by playing chords.

Once we got to the sixties with the advent of free music, the whole business of how to play the piano, whether in ensemble or solo, had to be reconsidered from top to bottom. I realized that it was not necessary to use the old models. In fact, one would have to invent a way to play this instrument, because since bebop, piano had been pretty much a one-handed instrument.

What's the role of piano in free music? My first stab at solo piano in 1972, at Manfred Eicher's suggestion, was just after my synthesizer period. I demanded that the acoustic piano give me the long sustained notes that I could get so easily with a synth. To do this required close miking and the patience to let a phrase resonate until all the overtones were sounded. Manfred used close miking and reverb, which gave me an original style from that first solo piano recording.

Electricity allowed one to play a lot slower than had been previously played, and with sequencers and sample-and-hold modules, one could play a lot faster than anyone had ever played on the piano. So electricity threw down the gauntlet. Can you play as fast as a synthesizer? Can you play as slow as the electric instruments? And for the next two decades, I spent time playing very slow and very fast.

Jimmy Giuffre believed in several linear voices rather than chords and linear. Linear voices changed the very meaning of harmony. With solo piano there was the alternative possibility to play all the notes of the melody at once, because when you play a melody, if you think of it vertically, instead of horizontally it becomes a chord.

When you play with a band, there are many questions about how to harmonize with musicians who are playing microtonally. You do that with the overtones. This whole business of letting things sustain suggested a whole new way of playing the piano.

The only thing we needed to know about the future of solo piano music was what not to do, and that was: what was being done before. The decisions about what to do are still completely open and there are no precedents. One of the reasons I record a lot is that the answers are still not in.

Postscript

This is one of the world's great hotels.
I'm dining at one of the world's finest restaurants.
I'm playing at one of the world's great jazz festivals,
and I'm listening to Lee Konitz, one of the world's
great saxophonists.
How'm I ever gonna play the blues?

Fax from Paul Bley, 8 July 1998
Istanbul Festival, Ciragan Palace Kempinski Hotel
Istanbul, Turkey

Bibliography

Carr, Ian, Digby Fairweather & Brian Priestley. *Jazz: The Essential Companion*. London: Grafton Books, 1987.

Dobbin, Len. "Paul Bley: The Montreal Years," *Coda* magazine, June-July, 1965.

Fitzgerald, Michael, ed. "The Lenox School of Jazz." Web Site: http://www.eclipse.net/~fitzgera/lenox/lenhome.htm

Gilmore, John. *Swinging in Paradise: The Story of Jazz in Montreal*. Montreal: Véhicule Press, 1988.

Gilmore, John. *Who's Who of Jazz in Montreal: Ragtime to 1970*. Montreal: Véhicule Press, 1989.

Jones, LeRoi (Amiri Baraka). *Black Music*. New York: Wm. Morrow & Co., 1968.

Kallmann, Helmut, Gilles Potvin & Kenneth Winters, eds. *Encyclopedia of Music in Canada*. (Particularly the Paul Bley entry written by Mark Miller). Toronto/Buffalo/London: University of Toronto Press, 1994.

Kernfeld, Barry, ed. *The New Grove Dictionary of Jazz*. (Particularly the Paul Bley entry written by Ran Blake). New York: St. Martin's Press, 1994.

Kluck, Henk. *Bley Play: The Paul Bley Recordings*. Emmen, Netherlands: Henk Kluck, 1995.

Litweiler, John. *The Freedom Principle: Jazz After 1958*. New York: William Morrow & Co., 1984.

Marsh, James. H., editor in chief. *The Canadian Encyclopedia*. Edmonton: The Hurtig Publishers, 1985.

Meeker, David. *Jazz in the Movies*. New York: Da Capo Press, 1981.

Miller, Mark. *Boogie, Pete & the Senator. Canadian Musicians in Jazz: he Eighties*. Toronto: Nightwood Editions, 1987.

Miller, Mark. *Cool Blues: Charlie Parker in Canada 1953*. London, Ontario: Nightwood Editions, 1989.

Miller, Mark. *Jazz in Canada: Fourteen Lives.* Toronto: Nightwood Editions, 1988.

Smith, Bill. "Paul Bley," *Coda* magazine #166, April–May 1979.

Spellman, A.B. *Black Music: Four Lives.* New York: Schocken Books, 1970.

Wilmer, Val. *As Serious as Your Life.* Westport, CT: Lawrence Hill & Co., 1980.

Selected Discography

For a more complete annotated discography, access Henk Kluck's Bley discography through www.improvart.com/bley/.

Format used in this discography: Artist credit, personnel, location and date of recording, label name and number, album title.

Abbreviations used: as (alto saxophone), b (bass), b–cl (bass clarinet), bar–s (baritone saxophone), cl (clarinet), d (drums), el–g (electric guitar), el–c (electric clarinet), el–cello (electric cello), el–p (electric piano), el–vb (electric vibraphone), fl (flute), fl–h (fluegelhorn), g (guitar), org (organ), p (piano), perc (percussion), syn (synthesizer), ss (soprano saxophone), tb (trombone), tp (trumpet), ts (tenor saxophone), v (violin), vb (vibraphone), voc (vocal).

All albums listed are issued in the US unless indicated as follows: CND (Canadian), CZ (former Czechoslovakia), DK (Denmark), EU (Europe), F (France), G (Germany), I (Italy), J (Japan), UK (United Kingdom), SW (Switzerland)

PAUL BLEY
Paul Bley (p), other personnel unknown
1952, Montreal
Silver (unissued), *Like the Moon Above You*

PAUL BLEY TRIO
Paul Bley (p), Oscar Pettiford, (b), Kenny Clarke (drums)
1952, New York
Stinson (unissued)

JAZZ WORKSHOP
Paul Bley (p), Neil Michaud (b), Dick Garcia (g), Brew Moore (ts), Ted Paskert (d), Charlie Parker (as)
5 February 1953, CBC-TV, Montreal
Jazz Showcase 5003, *Charlie Parker All Stars: Bird on the Road*; Uptown UPCD 2619-82736 (CD), *Charlie Parker: Montreal 1953*

CHARLES MINGUS AND HIS ORCHESTRA
Paul Bley (conductor)
27 October 1953, New York
Debut EP 450 (45 rpm)

PAUL BLEY
Paul Bley (p), Charles Mingus (b), Art Blakey (d)
30 November 1953, New York
Debut DLP 7, *Introducing Paul Bley*

PAUL BLEY TRIO
Paul Bley (p), Percy Heath (b), Alan Levitt (d)
3 February 1954, New York
Emarcy MG 36092, *Paul Bley*

PAUL BLEY QUARTET
Paul Bley (p), Dave Pike (vb), Charlie Haden (b), Lennie McBrowne (d)
Fall 1957, Los Angeles
GNP Gene Norman Presents GNP 31, *Solemn Meditation*

PAUL BLEY QUINTET
Paul Bley (p), Ornette Coleman (as), Don Cherry (tp), Charlie Haden
(b), Billy Higgins (d)
October 1958, Hillcrest Club, Los Angeles
Inner City IC 1007, *Live at the Hillcrest Club*; Musidisc (F) 500542 (CD),
The Fabulous Paul Bley Quintet

GEORGE RUSSELL AND HIS ORCHESTRA
Bill Evans (p), Paul Bley (p) and others.
January 1960, New York
Affinity (UK) AFF 152, *Jazz in the Space Age*
Decca DL 9219 GRP 18262

CHARLES MINGUS GROUP
Charles Mingus (b), Jimmy Knepper (tb), Booker Ervin (ts), Lorraine
Cousins (voc), Ted Curson (tp), Joe Farrell (ts), Yuseef Lateef (fl, ts), Eric
Dolphy (as, b-cl, fl), Paul Bley (p), Danny Richmond (d)
25 May 1960, New York
Mercury MG 20627 (mono); Mercury SR 60627 (stereo)

CHARLES MINGUS GROUP
Charles Mingus (b), Lonnie Hillyer (tp), Charles McPherson (as), Paul
Bley (p), Dannie Richmond (d), Ted Curson (tp), Booker Ervin (ts),
Eric Dolphy (b-cl)
11 November 1960, New York
Candid CCD 79026 (CD), *Reincarnation of a Love Bird*

JIMMY GIUFFRE 3
Jimmy Giuffre (cl, ts), Paul Bley (p), Steve Swallow (b)

3 March 1961, New York
ECM 21438-2 (2–CDs, 1961
Verve V8397 (mono), *Fusion*

DON ELLIS – STEVE SWALLOW – PAUL BLEY
Don Ellis (tp), Steve Swallow (b), Paul Bley (p)
21 April 1961, New York
Candin CCD 79032 (CD), *Out of Nowhere*

JIMMY GIUFFRE 3
Jimmy Giuffre (cl), Paul Bley (p), Steve Swallow (b)
August 1961, New York
ECM 21438-2 (2 CDs), 1961
Verve V8402 (mono), *Thesis*

JIMMY GIUFFRE 3
Jimmy Giuffre (cl), Paul Bley (p), Steve Swallow (b)
23 November 1961, Bremen, Germany
hat ART (SW) CD 6071 (CD), *Flight, Bremen 1961*

DON ELLIS QUARTET
Don Ellis (tp), Paul Bley (p), Gary Peacock (b), Gene Stone (d), Nick Martinis (d)
15 & 17 July 1962, Hollywood
Pacific ST 55 (stereo), *Essence*

PAUL BLEY TRIO
Paul Bley (p), Steve Swallow (b), Pete LaRoca (d)
17 August 1962, Newark, NJ
Savoy SJL 1148, Floater; BYG (F) 529 114, *Footloose*

JIMMY GIUFFRE 3
Jimmy Giuffre (cl), Paul Bley (p), Steve Swallow (b)
10 October 1962, New York
Columbia CS 8764 (stereo), *Free Fall*

PAUL BLEY TRIO
Paul Bley (p), Gary Peacock (b), Paul Motian (d)
13 April 1963, New York
ECM (G) 1003 (843 162-2) (CD) *With Gary Peacock*
ECM 78118-21003-2 (CD), *With Gary Peacock*

SONNY ROLLINS QUARTET WITH COLEMAN HAWKINS
Sonny Rollins (ts), Paul Bley (p), Bob Cranshaw (b), Roy McCurdy (d),

guest: Coleman Hawkins (ts)
15 July 1963, New York
Bluebird 2179-2RB (CD), *All the Things You are, 1963-1964*; RCA Victor
LSP 2712, *Sonny Meets Hawk*

PAUL BLEY TRIO
Paul Bley (p), Steve Swallow (b), Pete LaRoca (d)
12 September 1963
Newark, NJ
Savoy MG 12182, *Footloose*; Savoy SJL 1175, *Syndrome*

PAUL BLEY QUARTET
Paul Bley (p), John Gilmore (ts), Gary Peacock (b), Paul Motian (d)
9 March 1964, New York
Improvising Artists Inc. IAI 37 38 41, *Turning Point*

PAUL BLEY QUINTET
Paul Bley (p), Dewey Johnson (tp), Marshall Allen (as), Eddie Gomez
(b), Milford Graves (d)
20 October 1964, New York
ESP Disk 1008, *Barrage*

JAZZ COMPOSERS ORCHESTRA
Paul Bley (p), Eddie Gomez (b), Milford Graves (d), Steve Lacy (ss),
Jimmy Lyons (as), Mike Mantler (tp), Fred Pirtle (bar-s), Roswell Rudd
(tb), Willie Ruff (fr-h), Archie Shepp (ts)
29 December 1964, New York
ECM 841124-2 (CD), *Communication*

PAUL BLEY TRIO
Paul Bley (p), Steve Swallow (b), Barry Altschul (perc)
20 May & 18 December 1965
ESP CD 1021-2 (CD), *Closer*

PAUL BLEY TRIO
Paul Bley (p), Kent Carter (b), Barry Altschul (d)
5 November 1965, Copenhagen
Arista Al 1901 (2 LPs), *Copenhagen and Haarlem*

PAUL BLEY TRIO
Paul Bley (p), Mark Levinson (b), Barry Altschul (d)
1 July 1966, Rome
Red Records (I) VPA 117, *Ramblin' with Paul Bley*

PAUL BLEY TRIO
Paul Bley (p), Mark Levinson (b), Barry Altschul (d)
21 September & 4 October 1966, Baarn, Netherlands
Fontana (J) PHCE 1006 (CD), *Blood*

PAUL BLEY TRIO
Paul Bley (p), Mark Levinson (b), Barry Altschul (d)
5 September 1966, Prague
Suprahon (CZ) SUA 15487, *Live Recordings of the International Jazz Festival
Praha '66*

BARRY ALTSCHUL – PAUL BLEY GARY PEACOCK
Barry Altschul (d), Paul Bley (p), Gary Peacock (b)
29 June 1967, New York City
Improvising Artists Inc. IAI 37 38 44, *Virtuosi*

PAUL BLEY TRIO
Paul Bley (p), Gary Peacock (b), Barry Altschul (d)
28 July 1967, New York
ECM (G) 1010 ST, *Ballads*

PAUL BLEY TRIO
Paul Bley (p), Gary Peacock (b), Billy Elgart (d)
11 May 1968, Seattle
ECM 78118-21003-2 (CD), *With Gary Peacock*

PAUL BLEY TRIO
Paul Bley (p), Mario Pavone (b), Barry Altschul (d)
4 December 1968, Montreal
CBC (CND) RCI 305, Canada; Radio Canada International (CND)
ACM 38 CD 1-4 (4 CDs), *Anthology of Canadian Music: Jazz*

BLEY – PEACOCK SYNTHESIZER SHOW
Paul Bley (Moog syn, RMI el-p), Annette Peacock (el-vb, voc, syn),
Perry Robinson (el-cl), Glenn Moore (b), Laurence Cook (d)
6 April 1969, New York
Polydor (EU) 244.046, *Revenge: The Bigger the Love, the Greater the Hate*;
Polydor (UK) 2425-043

PAUL BLEY SYNTHESIZER SHOW
Paul Bley (ARP syn, RMI el-p, p), Richard Youngstein (b), Steve Haas (d)
9 December 1970, New York
Milestone MSP 9033, *Synthesizer Show*

ANNETTE PEACOCK
Annette Peacock (voc, claviers, vib), Paul Bley (syn, p), Glenn Moore (b), Laurence Cook (d)
1971, New York
RCA Victor LSP 4578, *I'm the One*

PAUL BLEY SYNTHESIZER SHOW
Paul Bley (AARP syn, RMI el-p, p), Glenn Moore (b), Steve Haas (d)
21 January 1971, New York
Milestone MSP 9033, *Synthesizer Show*

PAUL BLEY – ANNETTE PEACOCK SYNTHESIZER SHOW
Paul Bley (ARP syn, RMI el-p), Annette Peacock (voc, el-p, p, syn), Han Bennink (d)
26 March 1971, Rotterdam
Polydor (UK) 2383.105, *Dual Unity*

PAUL BLEY SOLO
Paul Bley (p)
11 September 1972, Oslo
ECM 78118-21023-2 (CD), *Open, to Love*

PAUL BLEY AND SCORPIO
Paul Bley (p, Fender & RMI el-p, ARP syn), Dave Holland (b, fuzz pedal), Barry Altschul (perc)
22 October & 24 November, New York
Milestone (UK) M 9046, *Scorpio*

PAUL BLEY – NIELS-HENNING ØRSTED PEDERSEN
Paul Bley (p, el-p), Niels-Henning Ørsted Pederwen (b)
24 June 1973, Copenhagen
SteepleChase (DK) SCCD 31005 (CD), *Paul Bley/NHØP*

MARION BROWN
Marion Brown (as), Muhal Richard Abrams (org, el-p, p), Paul Bley (el-p), Steve McCall (d, perc), Bill Hasson (perc, narration)
7 May 1974, Boston
Impulse AS 9275, *Sweet Earth Flying*

JACO PASTORIUS – PAT METHENY – BRUCE DITMAS – PAUL BLEY
Jaco Pastorius (el-b), Pat Metheny (el-g), Bruce Ditmas (d), Paul Bley (d)
16 June 1974, New York
DIW (J) 32 DIW 312 CD (CD), *Jaco*

PAUL BLEY SOLO
Paul Bley (p)
8-9 August 1974, Oslo
DIW (J) DIW 319 (CD), *Alone Again*

PAUL BLEY – JIMMY GIUFFRE – BILL CONNORS
Paul Bley (p, el-p), Jimmy Giuffre (cl, ts, fl), Bill Connors (g)
November 1974, New York
Improvising Artists Inc. IAI 37 38 39, *Quiet Song*

PAUL BLEY – GARY PEACOCK – BARRY ALTSCHUL
Paul Bley (p, el-p), Gary Peacock (b), Barry Altschul (d, perc)
25 July 1976, Nemo No Sato, Japan
Improvising Artists Inc. IAI 37 38 49, *Japan Suite*

LEE KONITZ – PAUL BLEY – BILL CONNORS
Lee Konitz (as, ss), Paul Bley (p, el-p), Bill Connors (g, el-g)
11 June 1977, New York
Improvising Artists Inc. IAA 37 38 45, *Pyramid*

PAUL BLEY SOLO
Paul Bley (p)
1-3 July 1977, New York
Improvising Artists Inc. IAI 37 38 53, *Axis*

JIMMY GIUFFRE – LEE KONITZ – BILL CONNORS – PAUL
BLEY
Jimmy Giuffre (ss, fl), Paul Bley (p)
19 May 1978, San Francisco
Improvising Artists Inc. IAI 37 38 59, *IAI Festival*

RALPH SIMON
Ralph Simon (ss, ts), Paul Bley (p, el-p), John Scofield (g, el-g), David
Dunaway (b), Jabali Billy Hart (d), Tom Beyer (perc)
August 1980, New York
GramaVision Inc. GR 8002, *Time Being*

ALFED HARTH
Alfred Harth (ts, ss, as, b-cl), Paul Bley (p), Barre Phillips (b), Trilok
Gurtu (perc), Maggie Nicols (voc)
May 1983, Ludwigsburg, Germany
ECM (G) 1264 (815 334-1), *This Earth*

PAUL BLEY SOLO
Paul Bley (p)
19 May 1983, Paris
Owl (F) 034 CD 3800342 (CD), *Tears*

PAUL BLEY SOLO
Paul Bley (p)
21 May 1983, Milan
Soul Note (I) 121090-2 (CD), *Tango Palace*

PAUL BLEY – GEORGE CROSS McDONALD
Paul Bley (p), George Cross McDonald (perc)
22 May 1983
Milan
Soul Note (I) SN 1085, *Sonor*

PAUL BLEY TRIO
Paul Bley (p), Jesper Lundgaard (b), Aage Tanggaard (d)
26 February 1985, Copenhagen
SteepleChase (DK) SCCD 31205 (CD), *Questions*

CHET BAKER – PAUL BLEY
Chet Baker (tp, voc), Paul Bley (p)
27 February 1985, Copenhagen
SteepleChase SCH 31207 (CD), *Diane*

PAUL BLEY GROUP
Paul Bley (p), John Scofield (el-g), Steve Swallow (el-b), Barry Altschul
(d)
10 March 1985, New York
Soul Note (I) SN 1140 CD (CD), *Hot*

PAUL BLEY TRIO
Paul Bley (p), Jesper Lundgaard (b), Billy Hart (d)
8 December 1985, Copenhagen
SteepleChase (DK) SCCD 31214 (CD), *My Standard*

PAUL BLEY – JOHN SURMAN – BILL FRISELL – PAUL MOTIAN
Paul Bley (p), John Surman (ss, bs, b-cl), Bill Frisell (el-g), Paul Motian
(d)
15-17 January 1986, Oslo
ECM 21320-2 CD, *Fragments*

BOB MOVER TRIO
Bob Mover (as, ss), Paul Bley (p), John Abercrombie (el-g, g-syn)
22 January 1986, Montreal
Justin Time Records (CND) JUST 14, *The Night Bathers*

PAUL BLEY – JESPER LUNDGAARD
Paul Bley (p), Jesper Lundgaard (b)
26 March 1986, Copenhagen
SteepleChase (DK) SCCD 31223 (CD), *Live*; SteepleChase (DK) SCCD
31230 (CD), *Live Again*

PAUL BLEY – RON McCLURE – BARRY ALTSCHUL
Paul Bley (p), Ron McClure (b), Barry Altschul (d)
May 1987
SsteepleChase (DK) SCCD 31286, *Indian Summer*

PAUL BLEY – PAUL MOTIAN
Paul Bley (p), Paul Motian (perc)
3-4 July 1987, Milan
Soul Note (I) SN 1190 CD, *Notes*

PAUL BLEY QUARTET
Paul Bley (p), John Surman (ss, b-cl), Bill Frisell (el-g), Paul Motian (d)
November 1987, Oslo
ECM (G) 1365 (835 250-2) (CD), no title

PAUL BLEY SOLO
Paul Bley (p)
December 1987, Montreal
Justin Time Records (CND) JUST 28-2 (CD), *Solo*

DINO BETTI VAN DER NOOT GROUP/ORCHESTRA
Paul Bley (p) and others
1988-1989, Milan
Innowo (I) IN 813 (CD), *Space Blossoms*

PAUL BLEY GROUP
Paul Bley (p), John Abercrombie (el-g), Red Mitchell (b), Barry Altschul
(d)
1-6 March 1988
Soul Note (I) 121235-2 (CD), *Live at Sweet Basil*

PAUL BLEY SOLO
Paul Bley (p)

2 April 1988, Copenhagen
SteepleChase (DK) SCCD 31236 (CD), *Solo Piano*

PAUL BLEY SOLO
Paul Bley (p)
April 1989, New York
American Clavé AMCL 1014 (2 CDs), *Darn It!*

PAUL BLEY SOLO
Paul Bley (p)
May 1989, Milan
Red Records (I) RR 123238-2 (CD), *Blues for Red*

PAUL BLEY – MICHAL URBANIAK – RON McCLURE – BARRY
ALTSCHUL
Paul Bley (p), Michal Urbaniak (v), Ron McClure (b), Barry Altschul (d)
31 May 1989, New York
SteepleChase (DK) SCCD 31274 (CD), *Rejoicing*

CHARLIE HADEN WITH PAUL BLEY AND PAUL MOTIAN
Charlie Haden (b), Paul Bley (p), Paul Motian (d)
7 July 1989, Montreal
Verve (F) 523 259-2 (CD), *The Montreal Tapes*

FRANZ KOGLMANN
Paul Bley (p) and others
13–17 November 1989, Vienna
hat ART (SW) CD 6048 (CD), *A White Line*

PAUL BLEY TRIO
Paul Bley (p), Ron McClure (b), Billy Hart (d)
21 November 1989
SteepleChase (DK) SCCD 31246 (CD), *The Nearness of You*

PAUL BLEY – JIMMY GIUFFRE – STEVE SWALLOW
Paul Bley (p), Jimmy Giuffre (ss, cl), Steve Swallow (el-b)
16 December 1989, New York
Owl (F) 059 CD 3800592 (CD), *The Life of a Trio: Saturday*

PAUL BLEY – JIMMY GIUFFRE – STEVE SWALLOW
Paul Bley (p), Jimmy Giuffre (ss, cl), Steve Swallow (el-b)
17 December 1989, New York
Owl (F) 060 CD 3800602 (CD), *The Life of a Trio: Sunday*

PAUL BLEY – GARY PEACOCK
Paul Bley (p), Gary Peacock (b)
18 December 1989, New York
Owl (F) 058 CD 3800582 (CD), *Partners*

PAUL BLEY TRIO
Paul Bley (p), Bob Cranshaw (b), Keith Copeland (d)
22 December 1989
SteepleChase (DK) SCCD 31259 (CD), *Bebop*

GARY BURTON – PAUL BLEY
Gary Burton (vb), Paul Bley (p)
29 March 1990, Copenhagen
GNP Crescendo GNPC 2204, *Right Time, Right Place*
Sonet Records (UK) SNTCD 1038 (CD), *Right Time, Right Place*

FREDRIK LUNDIN QUINTET FEATURING PAUL BLEY
7-8 April 1990, Copenhagen
Stunt Records STUCD 19002 (CD), *Pieces of...*

PAUL BLEY – HANS KOCH – FRANZ KOGLMANN
Paul Bley (p), Hans Koch (cl, s), Franz Koglmann (fl-h)
23-24 May 1990, Boswill, Switzerland
hat ART (SW) CD 6081 (CD), *Paul Bley 12 (+6) in a Row*

PAUL BLEY – CHARLIE HADEN – PAUL MOTIAN
Paul Bley (p), Charlie Haden (b), Paul Motian (d)
27 July 1990, Milan
Soul Note (I) 121240-2 (CD), *Memoirs*

JON BALLANTYNE – PAUL BLEY
Jon Ballantyne (p), Paul Bley (p)
February 1991, Montreal
Justin Time Records (CND) JUST 39-2 (CD), *A Musing*; Justin Time
Records (CND) JUST 40-2 (CD), *Changing Hands*

PAUL BLEY – TIZIANA GHIGLIONI
Paul Bley (p), Tiziana Ghiglioni (voc)
6 March 1991, Milan
Splasc(h) (I) CD H348-2 (CD), *Lyrics*

IVO PERELMAN
Ivo Perelman (ts), Paul Bley (p)
22 May & 9-11 July 1991, New York
ENJA (G) ENJ 7005-2 (CD), *Children of Ibeji*

JOHN SURMAN – PAUL BLEY – GARY PEACOCK – TONY OXLEY
John Surman (bar-s, ss, b-cl), Paul Bley (p), Gary Peacock (b), Tony Oxley (d)
September 1991, Oslo
ECM (G) 1488 C517469-2 (CD), *In the Evenings Out There+3*

PAUL BLEY – MARC JOHNSON – JEFF WILLIAMS
Paul Bley (p), Marc Johnson (b), Jeff Williams (d)
December 1991, Denmark
SteepleChase (DK) SCCD 31303 (CD), *Paul Bley Plays Carla Bley*

PAUL BLEY – FRANZ KOGLMANN – GARY PEACOCK
Paul Bley (p), Franz Koglmann (fl-h, tp), Gary Peacock (b)
12-14 April 1992, Germany
hat ART (SW) CD 6118 (CD), *Annette*

PAUL BLEY
Paul Bley (p)
18 April 1992, Denmark
SteepleChase (DK) SCCD 31316 (CD), *Caravan Suite*

JIMMY GIUFFRE – PAUL BLEY – STEVE SWALLOW
Jimmy Giuffre (ss, cl, voc), Paul Bley (p), Steve Swallow (el-b)
25 April 1992, New York
Owl (F) 068 CD 3800682 (CD), *Fly Away Little Bird*

PAUL BLEY – GIKO PAVAN – MAURO BEGGIO
Paul Bley (p), Giko Pavan (b), Mauro Beggio (d)
1992, Mestre, Italy
Gala (I) CDGLP91046 (CD), *One Year After*

KESHAVAN MASLAK WITH PAUL BLEY
Keshavan Maslak (as, ts,cl voc), Paul Bley (p)
8-10 October 1992, Milan
Black Saint (I) 120149-2, *Not to be a Star*

PAUL BLEY SOLO
Paul Bley (p)
5 November 1992, Copenhagen
SteepleChase SCCD 31348 (CD), *At the Copenhagen Jazz House*

KESHAVAN MASLAK WITH PAUL BLEY
Keshavan Maslak (as, ts, cl), Paul Bley (p)

12-13 February 1993, Fort Lauderdale, Florida
Leo Records (UK) CD LR 104 (CD), *Romance in the Big City*

PAUL BLEY TRIO
Paul Bley (p), Steve Swallow (el-b), Paul Motian (d)
1 March 1993, New York
Transheart (J) TDCN 5081, *Zen Palace*

PAUL BLEY SOLO
Paul Bley (p)
2 March 1993
Transheart (J) TDCN 5084 (CD), *Hands On*

HANS LÜDEMANN – PAUL BLEY
Hans Lüdemann (p), Paul Bley (p)
21 March 1993, Köln, Germany
West Winds (G) WW 2085 (CD), *Moving Hearts*

PAUL BLEY TRIO
Paul Bley (p), Jay Anderson (b), Adam Nussbaum (d)
April 1993, Copenhagen
SteepleChase (DK) SCCD 31344 (CD), *If We May*

LEE KONITZ
Lee Konitz (ss, as), Jimmy Giuffre (cl), Paul Bley (p), Gary Peacock (b)
21 June 1993
Paddle Wheel (EUR) KICJ 174 (CD), *Rhapsody*

PAUL BLEY
Paul Bley (p, syn)
23-24 August 1993 and 1 September 1993, New York
Postcards (USA) POST 1001 (CD), *Synth Thesis*

PAUL BLEY SOLO
Paul Bley (p)
29 August 1993, Montreal
Justin Time Records (CND) JUST 56-2 (CD), *Sweet Time*

PAUL BLEY – JANE BUNNETT
Paul Bley (p), Jane Bunnett (ss, fl)
30 August 1993, Montreal
Justin Time Records (CND) JUST 58-2 58-2 (CD), *Double Time*

PAUL BLEY – TONY OXLEY – FURIO DICASTRI
Paul Bley (p), Tony Oxley (d), Furio di Castri (b)
28-29 March 1994, Milan
Soul Note 121285-2 (CD), *Chaos*

PAUL BLEY – SONNY GREENWICH
Paul Bley (p), Sonny Greenwich (g)
8 July 1994, Montreal
Justin Time Records (CND) JUST 69-2 (CD), *Outside In*

PAUL BLEY TRIO
Paul Bley (p, DX-7), David Eyges (el-cello), Bruce Ditmas (d)
17 September 1994, New York
Venus Records (J) TKCV 79074, *Modern Chant: Inspiration from Gregorian Chant*
Venus Records (J) TKCV 79084, *Emerald Blue: Inspiration from Gregorian Chant*

BRUCE DITMAS – PAUL BLEY – JOHN ABERCROMBIE–
DOMINE RICHARDS
Bruce Ditmas (d), Paul Bley (p), John Abercrombie (el-g), Domine Richards (b)
1995, New York
Postcards (USA) POST 1007 (CD), *What If*

PAUL BLEY – EVAN PARKER – BARRE PHILLIPS
Paul Bley (p), Evan Parker (ts, ss), Barre Phillips (b)
1995, Munich
ECM (G) ECM 1535 523 819-2 (CD), *Time Will Tell*

PAUL BLEY – HERBIE SPANIER – GEORDIE MCDONALD
Paul Bley (p), Herbie Spanier (t, fl-h, pt), Geordie McDonald (d)
1995, Montreal
Justin Time (CND) JUST 57-2 (CD), *Know Time*

SATOKO FUJI – PAUL BLEY
Satoko Fuji (p), Paul Bley (p)
1995, New York
LIBRA (USA) 202-003 (CD), *Something About Water*

KENNY WHEELER – PAUL BLEY
Kenny Wheeler (t), Paul Bley (p)
1996, Montreal
Justin Time Records (CND) JUST 97-2 (CD), *Touché*

RALPH SIMON AND THE MAGIC CLUB
Ralph Simon (ss, syn), Paul Bley (p, syn), Gary Peacock (b), Julian Priester (tb), Bruce Ditmas (d, syn), Alan Pasqua (p), Jeff Berman (vb), Tom Beyer (d), Elizabeth Panzer (h), Michael DiSibio (t)
1996 New York
Postcards (USA) POST 1015 (CD), *Music for the Millenium*

PAUL BLEY – GARY PEACOCK
Paul Bley (p), Gary Peacock (b)
1997, Milan
Soul Note (I) 121213-2 (CD), *Mindset*

GEORDIE MCDONALD – PAUL BLEY – RON ALLEN – ROB PITCH – DAVE PITCH
Geordie McDonald (perc), Paul Bley (p), Ron Allen (fl, s), Rob Pitch (el-g), Dave Pitch (b)
1998, Toronto
Sonavista (CDN) SV010 (CD), *Out in the Open*

PAUL BLEY
Paul Bley (p)
1998, Paris
BMG (F) 74321559342 (CD), *Jazz'n (e)motion*

PAUL BLEY – JAY ANDERSON – JEFF HIRSHFIELD
Paul Bley (p), Jay Anderson (b), Jeff Hirshfield (d)
1998, New York
Steeplechase (DK) SCCD31437 (CD), *Notes on Ornette*

PAUL BLEY – GARY PEACOCK – PAUL MOTION
Paul Bley (p), Gary Peacock (b), Paul Motion (d)
1999, New York
ECM (G) ECM 1670 559 447-2 (CD), *Not Two, Not One*

STITCH WYNSTON – PAUL BLEY – MIKE MURLEY – GEOFF YOUNG
Stich Wynston (d, p, voc), Paul Bley (p), Mikey Murley (s), Geoff Young (g)
1999, Toronto
BUZZ (CDN) ZZ 76006 (CD), *Modern Surfaces*

PAUL BLEY – MASAHIKO TOGASHI
Paul Bley (p), Masahiko Togashi (d)
1999, Tokyo
Sony Music Entertainment SRCS2168, *Echo*

Véhicule Press

www.vehiculepress.com